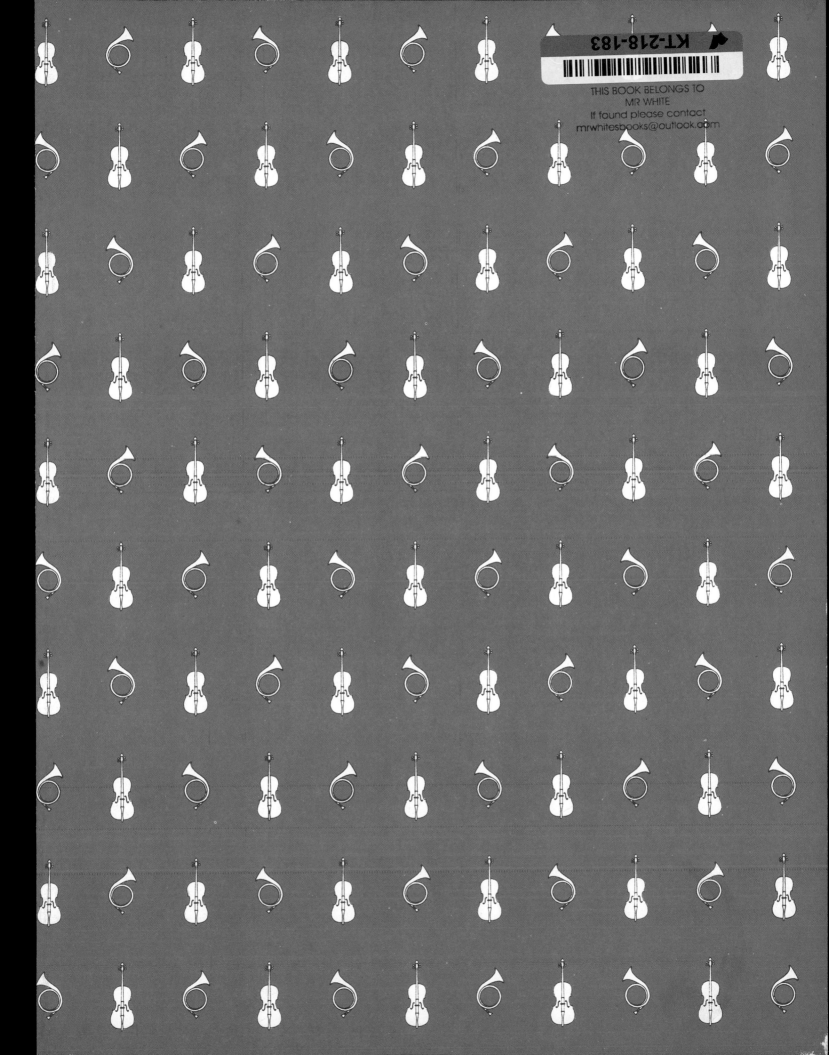

EYEWITNESS GUIDES

MUSIC

Tambourine

Triangle

19th-century Finnish *kantele*

Indian transverse flute

Four-keyed English flute, c. 1811

Moroccan lute with
feather plectrum

17th-century
German kit

19th-century German
ocarina (vessel flute)

Pellet drum

19th-century
Chinese *sihu*
(spike fiddle)
and bow

Tuba mouth-piece

Horn and trumpet mouth-pieces

EYEWITNESS 👁 GUIDES

MUSIC

Written by
NEIL ARDLEY

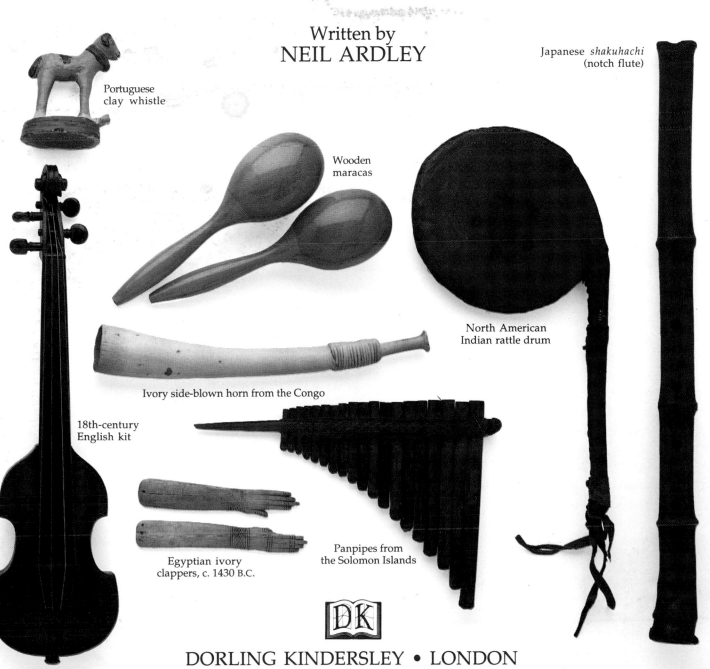

Portuguese clay whistle

Japanese *shakuhachi* (notch flute)

Wooden maracas

North American Indian rattle drum

Ivory side-blown horn from the Congo

18th-century English kit

Egyptian ivory clappers, c. 1430 B.C.

Panpipes from the Solomon Islands

DK

DORLING KINDERSLEY • LONDON

19th-century post horn

Double reeds

Black Sea fiddle, from
Georgia, Russia, c. 1865

Project Editor Janice Lacock

Editor Jane Elliot

Art editor Carole Ash

Photography Dave King, Phillip Dowell, Mike Dunning

Managing art editor Jane Owen

Managing editor Vicky Davenport

First published in Great Britain in 1989
by Dorling Kindersley Limited,
9 Henrietta Street, London WC2E 8PS

Bedouin *zummara*
(double "clarinet")
from Saudi Arabia

British Library Cataloging in publication Data
Ardley, Neil
Music
1. Music instruments
I. Title   II. Series
781.91

ISBN 0-86318-339-5

Colour reproduction by Colourscan, Singapore
Typeset by Windsorgraphics, Wimborne, Dorset
Printed in Italy by A. Mondadori Editore, Verona

Single reeds

Treble recorder,
early 18th century

Contents

Castanets

18th century
French flageolet

Seeing sound

T HE WORLD OF MUSIC is a kaleidoscope of sound. With most instruments it is easy to see how the different types of sound are made. Blowing a flute obviously gives a totally different sound from banging a drum. But you do not have to watch people playing to tell a flute from a drum, or any other instrument - you can recognize the sounds. Playing an instrument makes part of it vibrate rapidly to and fro. The vibration produces soundwaves in the air, which travel to our ears. The waves are small, but they cause rapid changes in air pressure at the same rate as the vibration of the instrument. The sound wave-from each instrument has its own kind of pressure changes. These can be shown by curved and jagged lines that are called wave forms (right). Each waveform is created by a particular pattern of vibration in an instrument. The sound of music causes our eardrums to vibrate in the same pattern as the instruments being played. These vibrations are interpreted by the brain so that we can recognize which instrument is being played.

Medieval musicians shown outside a cathedral in a Flemish book of hours

TUNING FORK
A tuning fork makes a very pure sound. The prongs vibrate regularly, creating a sound with a curving waveform. The rate at which the peaks pass gives the pitch. Faster vibrations produce a higher note.

VIOLIN
The violin makes a bright sound that has a jagged waveform. The violin sound shown here has the same pitch as the tuning fork. As a result the peaks of the waves produced by the violin are the same distance apart, and pass at the same rate, as those produced by a tuning fork.

FLUTE
The flute is playing the same note as the tuning fork and violin. The waveform of its sound is more curved than jagged, because the flute produces a purer, more mellow sound than the violin, with only a touch of brightness. In spite of this difference, the peaks of the waveform are the same distance apart and pass at the same rate.

GONG
Hitting a gong or a cymbal makes it vibrate in an irregular pattern. The crashing sound has a jagged, random waveform. We hear such waveforms as a noise with little, or no, recognizable pitch.

COMBINED WAVES
When people play together, the soundwaves from their instruments combine. Our ears receive the combined sound waves, making the eardrums vibrate with a very complex sound pattern. Yet our brains are able to sort out the different instruments playing.

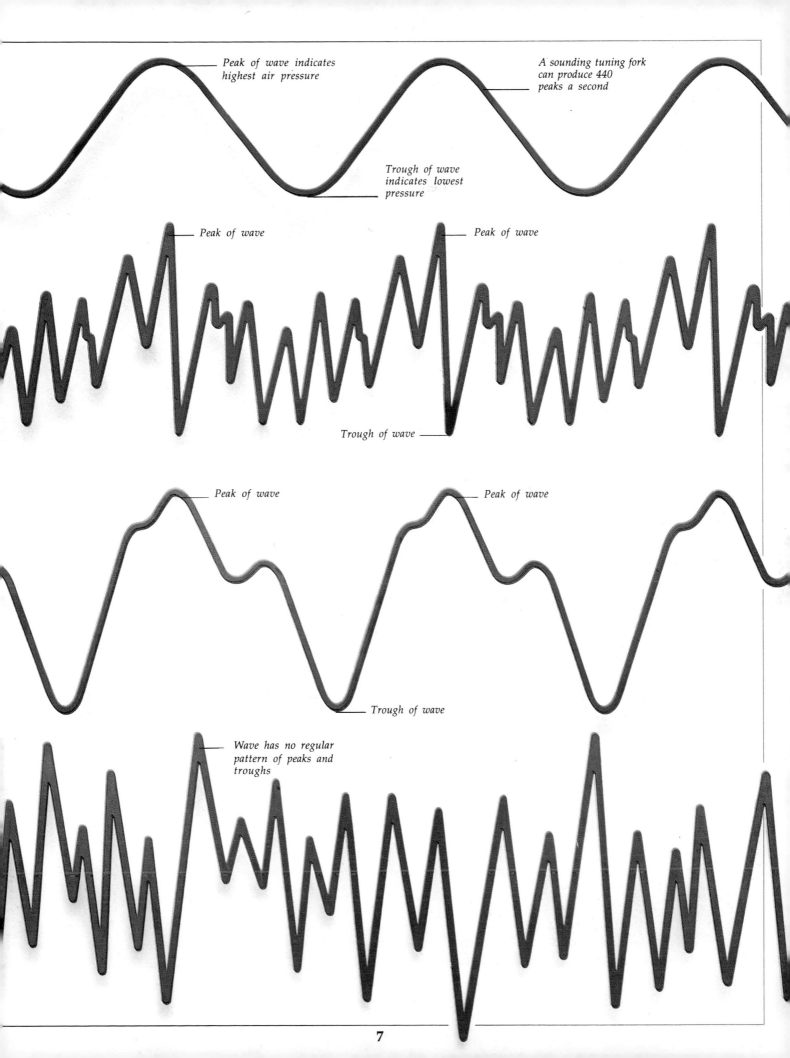

Peak of wave indicates highest air pressure

A sounding tuning fork can produce 440 peaks a second

Trough of wave indicates lowest pressure

Peak of wave

Peak of wave

Trough of wave

Peak of wave

Peak of wave

Trough of wave

Wave has no regular pattern of peaks and troughs

Wind tunnels

"AN ILL WIND THAT NOBODY BLOWS GOOD" is the parody of a proverb told about wind instruments. Learning some wind instruments, such as the saxophone, can produce an effect not unlike a cow in distress, but in good hands wind instruments can create a wonderful diversity of sounds. There are two main families of wind instruments: woodwind and brass. The materials mean nothing, as some woodwinds are made of brass, and some primitive brass instruments are made of wood. Both kinds of instruments are basically a hollow tube with a mouthpiece. Blowing into the mouthpiece makes the air inside the tube vibrate. The length of vibrating air is called the air column. Making it shorter raises the pitch, and the note sounds higher. Brass instruments, like the trumpet, have another way of raising the pitch. Blowing harder into the mouthpiece makes the air column split, so that it vibrates in two halves, three-thirds and so on, to give higher notes.

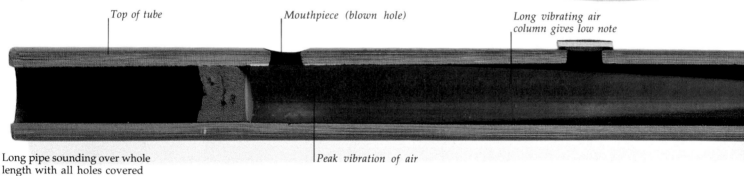

Top of tube

Mouthpiece (blown hole)

Long vibrating air column gives low note

Peak vibration of air

Long pipe sounding over whole length with all holes covered

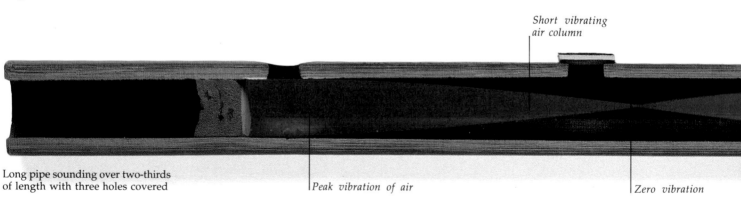

Short vibrating air column

Peak vibration of air

Zero vibration

Long pipe sounding over two-thirds of length with three holes covered

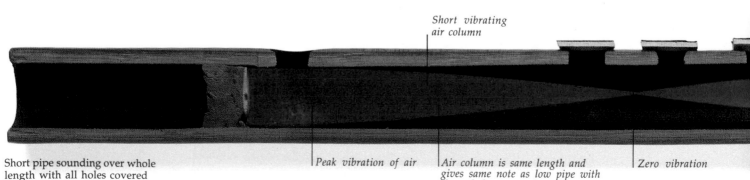

Short vibrating air column

Peak vibration of air

Air column is same length and gives same note as low pipe with three holes covered

Zero vibration

Short pipe sounding over whole length with all holes covered

Diverse mouthpieces

Woodwind and brass instruments are played with very different kinds of mouthpieces. Pipes and flutes simply have a hole that the player blows into, or across; this action sets the air column inside vibrating. Other woodwind instruments have mouthpieces with reeds. Here, blowing makes the reed vibrate and this sets the air column sounding. Brass instruments all have metal mouthpieces into which the player fits the lips. Blowing through the lips makes the mouthpiece vibrate, rather like a double reed.

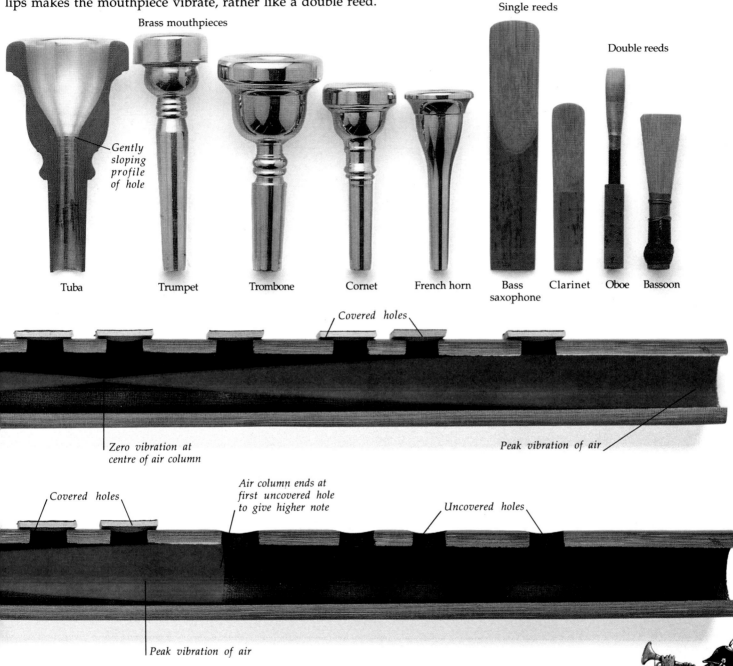

Brass mouthpieces

Single reeds

Double reeds

Gently sloping profile of hole

Tuba   Trumpet   Trombone   Cornet   French horn   Bass saxophone   Clarinet   Oboe   Bassoon

Covered holes

Zero vibration at centre of air column

Peak vibration of air

Covered holes

Air column ends at first uncovered hole to give higher note

Uncovered holes

Peak vibration of air

Covered holes

Peak vibration of air

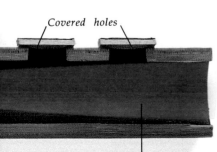

AIR COLUMNS
Blowing at the mouthpiece sets the air in woodwind or brass instruments vibrating. The vibration is greatest at the mouthpiece and at the other end of the tube. Moving inwards, the vibration lessens and ceases at the centre. The vibrating air sound also sets the body of the instrument vibrating, and this vibration sends out the sound waves (pp. 6 - 7). The length of the air column - from one peak of vibration to the next - gives the pitch of the note produced. Shortening the air column raises the pitch. This is done in woodwinds by uncovering holes in the tube, or by using a shorter instrument. Pressing the pistons in brass instruments makes the air column longer, so the pitch is lower. Brass players, (and to a lesser extent woodwind players) can make higher notes just by blowing harder. This splits up the air column so the vibration peaks are closer.

The Pied Piper lured children from Hamelin

Pipes and flutes

THE BREATHY, INTIMATE SOUND of pipes and flutes gives them a haunting quality. Perhaps this is why they have long been associated with magic - as in Mozart's opera *The Magic Flute*, and the legend of the Pied-Piper of Hamelin, whose music enchanted the children from the town. Sound is made simply by blowing across the end of an open pipe or a hole in the pipe (p. 8). This sets the air inside the pipe vibrating to give a lovely, mellow tone, to which the air escaping around the hole adds a distinctive hiss. Blowing harder into the pipe produces higher notes.

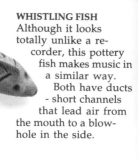

WHISTLING FISH
Although it looks totally unlike a recorder, this pottery fish makes music in a similar way. Both have ducts - short channels that lead air from the mouth to a blowhole in the side.

Notch

SEEING DOUBLE
Flageolets, a group of wind instruments that taper away from the mouthpiece-end, are often played in folk music. The tin whistle is an example. This intricately carved wooden instrument from Yugoslavia is a double flageolet with two pipes that can be played independently. It dates from about 1900, but the instrument has been known since the 1200s.

Blowholes   *Notch*

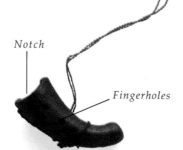

Fingerholes

Double set of fingerholes

Each pipe played by a different hand

Blowhole

EARLY MUSIC
Whistles made of reindeer toe-bones date from 40,000 B.C. These French bones may have been used to make signals rather than music.

MUSIC FROM FRUIT
This Sudanese whistle is made from a piece of gourd. It is played by blowing into a notch in the open end and closing the holes with fingers.

Lip-plate around blowhole

STONE ANIMALS
The frogs and eagle are unusual and attractive decorations on this 19th-century flageolet. It was carved in soapstone by the Haida Indians, a tribe who live on islands off Canada.

MUSIC OF THE GODS
Panpipes get their name from the myth of the Greek god Pan. When the nymph that Pan loved was turned into a reed, he cut the reed into a set of different length pipes, which he played to console himself. Today panpipes are most often associated with South American music.

ORIENTAL DESIGN
The notch cut in the end of the Japanese *shakuhachi* might make it easier to play than simple end-blown flutes such as the panpipes.

Elaborately carved wood in the shape of a dragon's head

Transverse flutes

Any pipe with a blown end or hole and fingerholes can be called a flute, but the name is usually given only to instruments that sound by blowing across a hole. These are classified as transverse, or side-blown, flutes and are held horizontally.

HANDY DEVICE

Although blown like a transverse flute, this bamboo instrument from Guyana is unusual in that the player changes the note by blocking and altering the shape of the large opening in the side with one hand.

Opening covered by the hand to change the note

Blowhole

Blowhole

Some pipes and flutes can be blown with the nose as well as the mouth

NOSE NOISE

Nose flutes are very common in the Pacific area. This beautifully decorated bamboo example comes from Fiji. It has a blowhole at each end and three fingerholes in the centre. The player blows with one nostril, blocking the other with his hand - or even tobacco!

THE BOEHM SYSTEM

The flute was greatly improved by the German instrument-maker Theobald Boehm (1794-1881), who invented a key system in which pads, operated by keys or the fingers, covered all the holes. This gave a better sound and made the flute easier to play.

HIGH NOTES

The piccolo is a small, high-pitched flute invented in the late 1700s. This early wooden example, c. 1800, has a single key. The modern instrument can be played by flautists because it has the same keywork as the concert flute.

Early wooden flute c. 1830

Fingerholes

Keys

Thumb keys

Keys for little fingers

Modern concert flute

FROM SIMPLICITY TO SOPHISTICATION

The concert flute, with its superior sound, ousted the recorder and flageolet in popularity during the 1800s. The simple keywork of the early wooden instrument contrasts with the complex keywork of the modern metal flute, but the modern instrument is easier to play and has a brighter sound.

Pads closed by fingers

Pads closed by keys

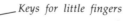

DRAGON FLUTE

The *lung ti*, or dragon flute, is an elegant and unusual Chinese transverse flute used in religious ceremonies. It is made of lacquered bamboo and has a thin sheet of paper covering the blowhole. This gives it a penetrating, buzzing sound, rather like a kazoo.

Ornate lacquer decoration

Vibrating reeds

This detail from a 17th-century painting shows two shawm players, accompanied by a trombonist, taking part in a festival procession in Spain

TO MAKE A HOLLOW CANE into a musical instrument, just cut a short length, flatten or slice through one end, and bore a few holes. Although it will produce little more than a squawk, this primitive pipe is the ancestor of all reed instruments. The distinctive, reedy sound is caused by a vibrating slice of cane called a beating reed. The result is a variety of sounds that range from the liquid notes of the clarinet, to the plaintive tones of the oboe, and the gruff blurts of the bassoon.

Clarinet reed

Mouthpiece

Barrel joint can be moved to adjust tuning

Head joint with keys for left hand

The normal position for a clarinet to be played

Single reeds

Clarinets and saxophones (p. 14) are played with a mouthpiece containing a metal ligature that holds in place a single reed. The player's mouth can influence the vibration of the reed to produce individual tones.

Keys for right little finger

Keys for left little finger

Middle joint with keys for right hand

Key for left thumb

Ring for neck sling

Cork ring to seal joints

The tube of a clarinet widens only at the bell

The soprano clarinet is the most played member of the clarinet family. This one is made of African blackwood

Keys for right index finger

Extra key to extend range

SHRILL BUT SWEET
Clarinets were developed during the 18th century, and the awkward keys were improved by Boehm (p. 11), about a century later. The name was inspired by the fact that the high notes suggested the sound of a trumpet or *clarino*. The sound, somewhat shrill and sweet, is widely used in orchestral music. A more lively, even wild, approach to playing the clarinet can be heard in traditional jazz and some folk music.

Holder for music stand

Right-hand rest

Keys for right thumb (fingerholes on other side)

Metal bell projects sound forward

Deep-sounding clarinets like this alto clarinet have a curved tube

Metal cap over bend in wooden tube

Bulbous bell gives the cor anglais its soft velvety sound

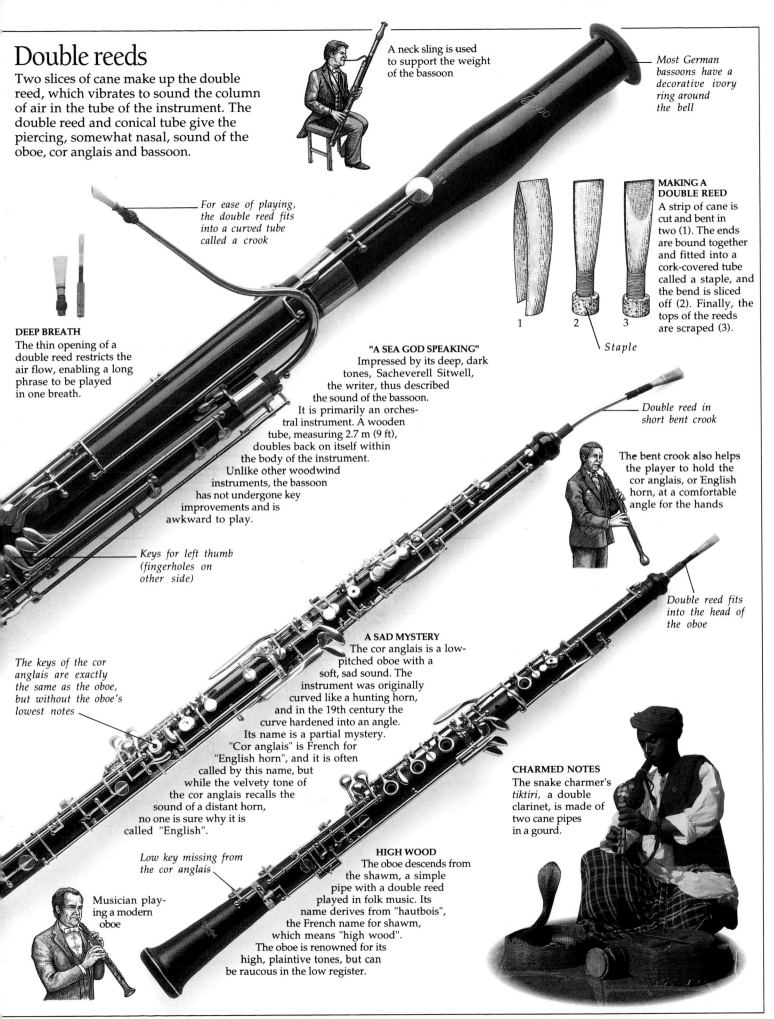

Double reeds

Two slices of cane make up the double reed, which vibrates to sound the column of air in the tube of the instrument. The double reed and conical tube give the piercing, somewhat nasal, sound of the oboe, cor anglais and bassoon.

A neck sling is used to support the weight of the bassoon

Most German bassoons have a decorative ivory ring around the bell

For ease of playing, the double reed fits into a curved tube called a crook

MAKING A DOUBLE REED
A strip of cane is cut and bent in two (1). The ends are bound together and fitted into a cork-covered tube called a staple, and the bend is sliced off (2). Finally, the tops of the reeds are scraped (3).

1   2   3

Staple

DEEP BREATH
The thin opening of a double reed restricts the air flow, enabling a long phrase to be played in one breath.

"A SEA GOD SPEAKING"
Impressed by its deep, dark tones, Sacheverell Sitwell, the writer, thus described the sound of the bassoon. It is primarily an orchestral instrument. A wooden tube, measuring 2.7 m (9 ft), doubles back on itself within the body of the instrument. Unlike other woodwind instruments, the bassoon has not undergone key improvements and is awkward to play.

Double reed in short bent crook

The bent crook also helps the player to hold the cor anglais, or English horn, at a comfortable angle for the hands

Keys for left thumb (fingerholes on other side)

The keys of the cor anglais are exactly the same as the oboe, but without the oboe's lowest notes

A SAD MYSTERY
The cor anglais is a low-pitched oboe with a soft, sad sound. The instrument was originally curved like a hunting horn, and in the 19th century the curve hardened into an angle. Its name is a partial mystery. "Cor anglais" is French for "English horn", and it is often called by this name, but while the velvety tone of the cor anglais recalls the sound of a distant horn, no one is sure why it is called "English".

Double reed fits into the head of the oboe

CHARMED NOTES
The snake charmer's *tiktiri*, a double clarinet, is made of two cane pipes in a gourd.

Low key missing from the cor anglais

Musician playing a modern oboe

HIGH WOOD
The oboe descends from the shawm, a simple pipe with a double reed played in folk music. Its name derives from "hautbois", the French name for shawm, which means "high wood". The oboe is renowned for its high, plaintive tones, but can be raucous in the low register.

13

Long-lasting hybrids

INVENTORS SELDOM GIVE THEIR NAMES to the instruments they create, but there are a few exceptions, such as the strangely named heckelphone and the sousaphone. But the most notable deviant is the saxophone. "Sax" is a common and appropriate name for the hybrid instrument that the Belgian inventor Adolphe Sax created in 1846. Combining a clarinet mouthpiece with oboe keywork, he fixed them to a conical brass tube with a slightly flared bell. The result was intended for military bands, which do contain saxophones, but the instrument has made its mark in popular music and jazz, due to its wide range of sounds and great powers of expression.

Mouthpiece with ligature holding single reed

Neck

Upper octave key

SAX SECTION
Big bands have a section of five saxophones - two altos, two tenors and a baritone sax. This is Count Basie's famous band, c.1958.

Key for left thumb

Lyre holder

BIG AND BEEFY
With its big beefy sound, the tenor sax is the most played of all the saxophones. Adolphe Sax made saxophones in 14 sizes, but only four are now common - the soprano, alto, tenor and baritone saxes. They make up a quartet, the saxophone equivalent of the string quartet.

Main body

Ring for sling

SAX STRIPPED BARE
This tenor saxophone has been stripped down to renew the gold lacquer coating that makes it gleam. The wide conical bore of the tube, which gives the sax a big sound, can be clearly seen.

Holder for right thumb to support body

Bell brace

Keys for the right little finger

Pillar on which key pivots

Toneholes produce big sound

Bell

Key guard

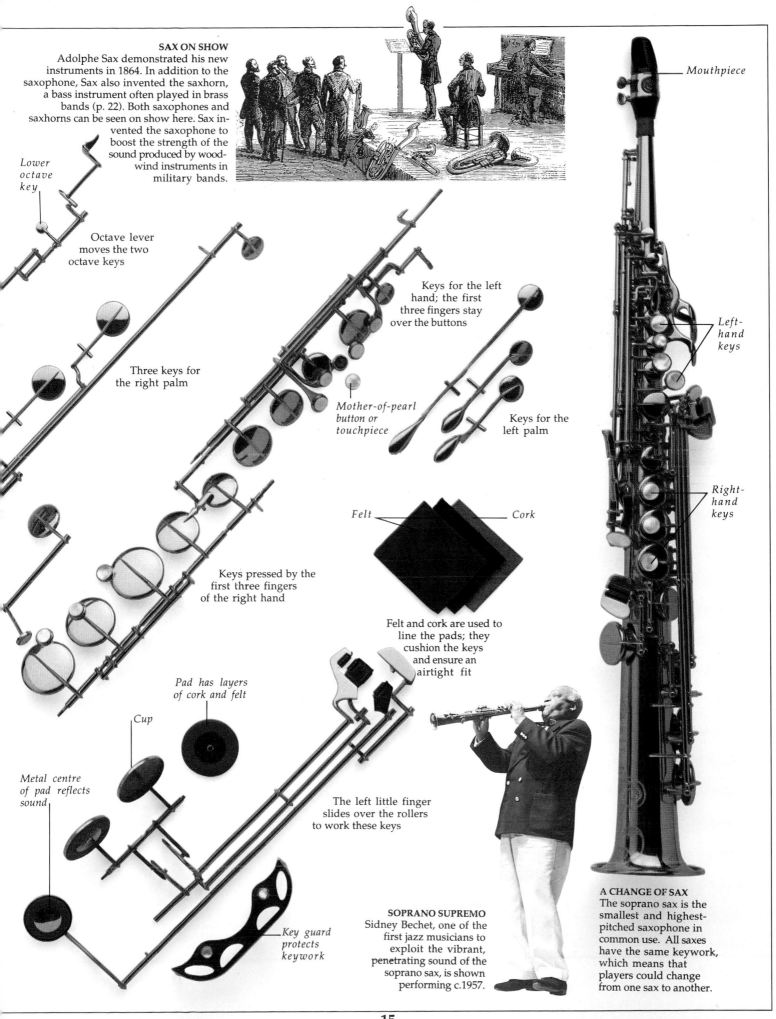

SAX ON SHOW
Adolphe Sax demonstrated his new instruments in 1864. In addition to the saxophone, Sax also invented the saxhorn, a bass instrument often played in brass bands (p. 22). Both saxophones and saxhorns can be seen on show here. Sax invented the saxophone to boost the strength of the sound produced by wood-wind instruments in military bands.

Mouthpiece

Lower octave key

Octave lever moves the two octave keys

Keys for the left hand; the first three fingers stay over the buttons

Three keys for the right palm

Mother-of-pearl button or touchpiece

Keys for the left palm

Left-hand keys

Right-hand keys

Felt

Cork

Keys pressed by the first three fingers of the right hand

Felt and cork are used to line the pads; they cushion the keys and ensure an airtight fit

Pad has layers of cork and felt

Cup

Metal centre of pad reflects sound

The left little finger slides over the rollers to work these keys

Key guard protects keywork

SOPRANO SUPREMO
Sidney Bechet, one of the first jazz musicians to exploit the vibrant, penetrating sound of the soprano sax, is shown performing c.1957.

A CHANGE OF SAX
The soprano sax is the smallest and highest-pitched saxophone in common use. All saxes have the same keywork, which means that players could change from one sax to another.

Bags of sound

TAKING A BREATH is a problem that faces all wind players. A few overcome it by the amazing feat of breathing in through the nose, and blowing out through the mouth at the same time. A more common solution is to separate the reed from the mouth, and activate the reed by squeezing a bag filled with air held under one arm, as in the bag-pipes. Accordions and harmonicas have free reeds; when blown by an air stream, these reeds vibrate to give a note without having a pipe. The result, in the case of bagpipes, is a strident, raucous sound, which is called a skirl.

A carved wooden goat's head is a traditional feature of central European bagpipes

Traditional 19th-century Scottish bagpiper

Drone

A BELLOWING GOAT
This ornately carved, bellows-blown bagpipe was made in Hungary in the early 20th century. The bellows are placed under the arm and pumped in and out to blow up the kidskin bag. The curved pipe contains a reed and sounds one continuous low note in the drone. The bag also blows a pair of reeds in the double chanter, which has fingerholes allowing both hands to play the melodies.

Air from the mouth of the goat's head blows the double chanter

The drone has a single beating reed and ends in a wide bell

The mouth pipe has a valve to prevent air leaving the bag

OLD WINDBAG
The *biniou* is a simple sheepskin bagpipe from Brittany in France. This instrument dates from the mid-19th century. The *biniou* is still played, often with a *bombard*, a type of shawm (p. 12), in performances of folk music. The piper blows into the mouth pipe to inflate the bag, which is then squeezed to sound the drone and chanter. Mouth-blown bagpipes of this kind are found throughout Europe, Africa and Asia. The sound of Scottish pipes, which have three drone pipes, is particularly distinctive.

Cleaning tool on chain

Bellows with straps to go around one arm

PEOPLE AT PLAY
A bagpipe features in this 16th-century painting by Breughel, who often portrayed people noisily enjoying themselves.

The single chanter is sounded by a double reed and has seven fingerholes

The bag is made of sheepskin

Pushing the knob opens the lower row of holes to sound extra notes

SUCK-AND-BLOW
The mouth organ, or the harmonica, has two sets of free reeds that sound as the player blows and sucks air through the instrument. Derived from Asian mouth organs, the harmonica dates back only to the last century.

Four of the 17 pipes are dummy pipes to balance the sheng

Fingerholes

Wind chamber

Mouthpiece

Band to hold the pipes together

FORM OF THE PHOENIX
The *sheng*, seen complete (far left) and in pieces (left and below), is a mouth organ that can be traced back 3,000 years to China. Its elegant shape is said to resemble the legendary bird, the phoenix. The *sheng* is played by blowing into, and sucking air from, the wind chamber, while fingering the holes in the pipes. Opening the holes admits air to the free reeds at the base of the bamboo pipes. The reeds are brass tongues that are weighted with wax to tune them.

A skilled Chinese musician, playing a complicated mouth organ

Lacquered wind chamber with holes for pipes

Brass tongues

Keys made of ivory and blue plastic

Bellows blow and suck air through the reeds

A 19th-century busker (street musician) with his monkey and accordion

SQUEEZE-AND-WHEEZE
Floral bellows, a nickel-plated grate, and blue plastic fittings add to the splendour of the accordion. While they are often associated with France, this 20th-century instrument was made in Italy. Pressing the keys and buttons admits air from the bellows to sets of free metal reeds. The accordion is supported by straps, leaving the hands free to operate the bellows and play the keys and buttons.

The wheezy sound of the reeds emerges from the grill

120 buttons give bass notes and chords

Piped music

THOUSANDS OF PIPES may send echoes through a great cathedral as the organ plays, yet the ancestor of the mighty pipe organ is the humble panpipe (p. 10). Pressing the organ keys sends air to an array of pipes that sound in the same way as woodwind pipes (pp. 8 - 9). The first organ, invented in Greece in c. 250 B.C., ingeniously used water power to blow the air through the pipes. Today electric fans do the job.

PORTABLE PIPES
The medieval portative organ could be carried about. One hand worked bellows to blow the air into a set of flue pipes. The other hand played the oddly-angled keys.

JUMBO PIPES
The lowest notes on a large organ may come from pipes almost 10 m (32 ft) long.

50% lead 50% tin

70% lead 30% tin

MIX OF METALS
Alloys of lead and tin are often used for organ pipes. Tin brightens the sound; lead dulls it.

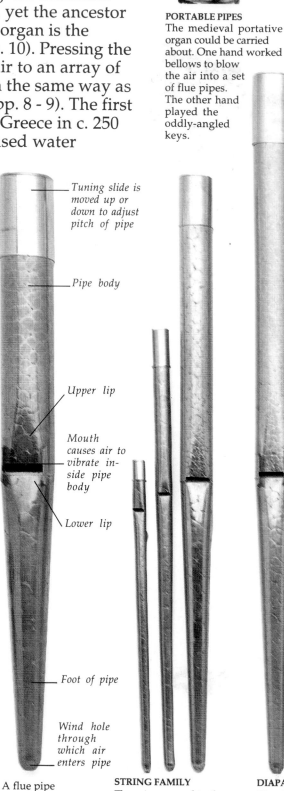

Tuning slide is moved up or down to adjust pitch of pipe

Pipe body

Upper lip

Mouth causes air to vibrate in-side pipe body

Lower lip

Foot of pipe

Wind hole through which air enters pipe

A flue pipe

STRING FAMILY
Flue pipes sound in the same way as a whistle (p. 10). These narrow pipes belong to the string family of organ pipes.

DIAPASON PIPES
"Ears", tiny metal flaps positioned each side of the "mouths" of the flue pipes, stabilize the sounds produced by the pipes.

Copper display diapason

DISPLAY PRINCIPAL
So-called because they are on view in the front of the organ, these pipes are made of 80% tin, giving a bright tone.

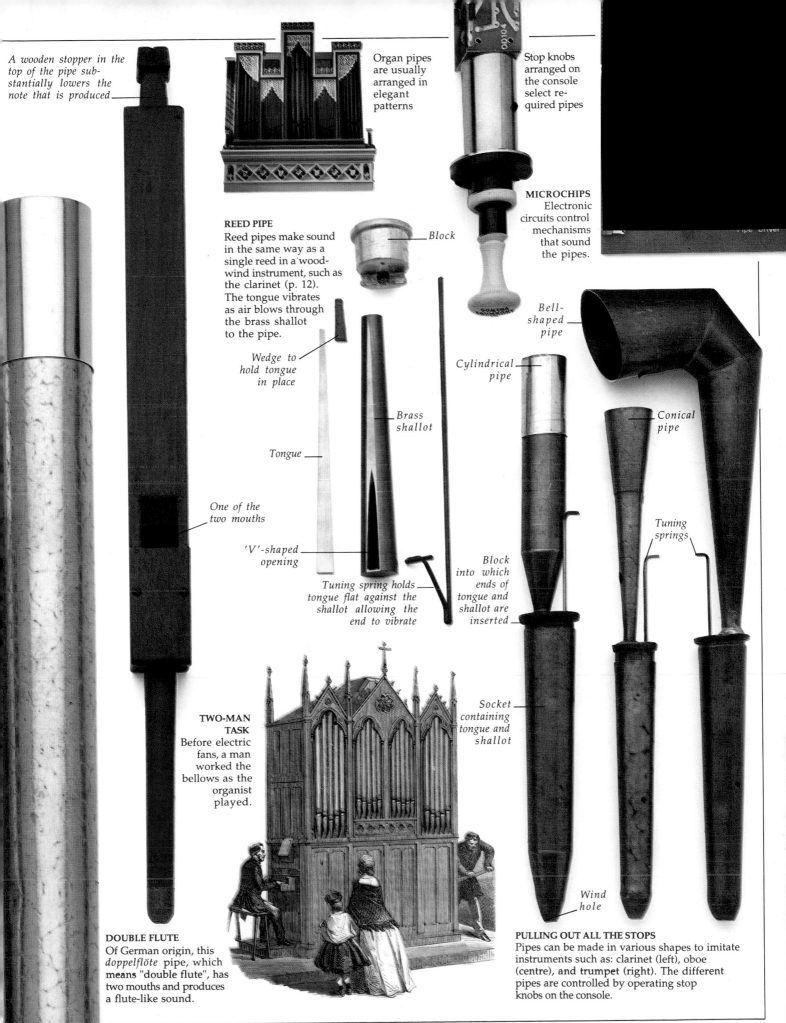

A wooden stopper in the top of the pipe substantially lowers the note that is produced

Organ pipes are usually arranged in elegant patterns

Stop knobs arranged on the console select required pipes

MICROCHIPS
Electronic circuits control mechanisms that sound the pipes.

REED PIPE
Reed pipes make sound in the same way as a single reed in a wood-wind instrument, such as the clarinet (p. 12). The tongue vibrates as air blows through the brass shallot to the pipe.

Block

Bell-shaped pipe

Cylindrical pipe

Conical pipe

Wedge to hold tongue in place

Brass shallot

Tongue

One of the two mouths

'V'-shaped opening

Tuning springs

Tuning spring holds tongue flat against the shallot allowing the end to vibrate

Block into which ends of tongue and shallot are inserted

TWO-MAN TASK
Before electric fans, a man worked the bellows as the organist played.

Socket containing tongue and shallot

Wind hole

DOUBLE FLUTE
Of German origin, this *doppelflöte* pipe, which **means** "double flute", has two mouths and produces a flute-like sound.

PULLING OUT ALL THE STOPS
Pipes can be made in various shapes to imitate instruments such as: clarinet (left), oboe (centre), and trumpet (right). The different pipes are controlled by operating stop knobs on the console.

Beginning of brass

AS THEIR NAME SUGGESTS, the principal brass instruments, such as the trumpet, trombone, horn and tuba, really are made of brass, usually lacquered or silver-plated for ease of cleaning. But they have their origin in natural instruments such as conch shells, hollowed branches and animal horns. In fact, any tube that can be sounded with the lips qualifies as a brass instrument, regardless of its material. Tubes are ideal for fanfares and hunting calls, but they can sound only a limited number of notes. In the attempt to extend their musical range, inventors came up with some bizarre contrivances including the aptly named serpent.

German musicians of 1520: the two on the left are playing shawms (p. 12) and the one on the right a trumpet

NOT THE KEY TO SUCCESS
Haydn composed his famous trumpet concerto of 1796 for the newly designed keyed trumpet as it could produce extra notes. However, the instrument was reputed to sound like "a demented oboe" so it did not long survive.

Carved mouthpiece

Double strap made from narrow strips of leather

NATURAL HORN
This East African instrument is fashioned from a gazelle horn. Even though the bony core has been removed and the outer layer of horn scraped away except at the mouthpiece, the elegant shape of the horn has been retained. It is blown from a carved opening at the side. In many parts of Africa horn bands give spectacular performances with side-blown horns.

The player puts his lips into the end of the tube

MADE BY AN INSECT
The inventive Aborigines have found an unusual way of making a *didjeridu*, their principal instrument - they bury a long eucalyptus branch in the ground so that termites bore out the middle. The hollow tube is then dug up, decorated with pigments and played by blowing down one end.

Funnel-shaped mouthpiece

FROM HUNTER TO POSTMAN
Small, curved horns used to sound signals during hunting were first described in France in the 14th century. When postal services began a century later, the postman used a similar post horn to announce his arrival and departure.

Carrying cord with decorative tassels

Detachable crook to
lengthen the tube,
thereby lowering all
the available notes

Cup-shaped
mouthpiece

REPTILE IMITATOR
It is obvious from its shape why this bizarre-looking
instrument was called a serpent when it was invented
in France in 1590. A cross between brass and woodwind,
its snake-like tube had two sets of fingerholes.

Left-hand
fingerholes

Placing one
hand in the
flared bell
raises a note

Right-hand
fingerholes

EXTRA CURLS
During the 17th century, in-
strument-makers gradually
lengthened the horn and
coiled it into a circle for ease
of playing. But the range of
notes the horn produced was
still limited until a century
later when detachable sections of tubing were
invented. Called crooks,
these lengthened the tube
and produced different sets
of notes. This typical
instrument has two crooks
and dates from 1780.

Italian horn, c. 1720

Two ways of playing
a serpent

Leather covering
painted to resemble
a serpent

Lizard-like creature
carved into the wood

Slender bell

RELIGIOUS MESSAGE
Fortunately for the player, this 1.5 m (5 ft) Moroccan trumpet is made
in sections of brass that can be taken apart after use. It is called a *nfîr*,
and is used to signal the end of the Muslim fast of Ramadan with long
blasts of sound. Trumpets like this date back to the Romans, who may
have introduced them into North Africa.

MOUNTAIN MUSIC
The sound of the long, wooden
alpenhorn has often resounded
through the Alps of Switzerland.
It was traditionally played by
herders but today is mainly a
tourist attraction.

Blazing brass

MODERN BRASS INSTRUMENTS in full cry, notably seried ranks of trumpets and trombones, can create a blaze of sound. This is not due just to the amount of effort that goes into blowing them, although purple faces may well accompany a thrilling fanfare. The brilliant sound that emanates is due to the narrow metal tube, cylindrical bore, and a wide, flared bell. Brilliance of tone, however, is only half the story. Blowing softly produces a mellow sound; using a mute lends the music a hint of mystery or even menace. Jazz musicians make full use of the different moods that can be created by the trumpet and trombone, playing them with great individuality to create exciting solos.

HERALDIC FANFARE
The herald shown in this German print of c. 1600 is playing an early trumpet. The instrument had no valves at this time.

Cup-shaped mouthpiece

Piston valves

Bore widens after valves

LEADER OF THE BAND
The mellow tones of the brass band are topped by the cornet, which leads the band and plays solo passages. It was invented by adding valves to the coiled post horn (p. 20). The cornet produces the same notes as the trumpet, and is played in the same way. It makes a fatter, less piercing, sound because the bore widens out more before the bell. But although the cornet may lack the trumpet's grandeur, it is easier to play.

TRADITIONAL SET-UP
Traditional jazz bands contain a trumpet and a trombone, as in Humphrey Lyttleton's band, shown here. Players aim to achieve a distinctively rough, even growling, sound.

SHOULDERING THE LOAD
The coils of this long and heavy 19th-century brass instrument enable the bandsman to carry it on his shoulder.

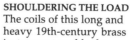

The water key vents water produced by condensation

Outer tube of slide

LOWERING THE TONE

A trumpet or cornet player can make a number of notes by pressing only three piston valves. Each valve contains holes that divert the vibrating air into a side-section of tubing. This lengthens the column of vibrating air in the instrument, and thus lowers the note. The side-sections are of medium, short, and long length. Combinations of the three valves give six notes below the note being sounded by the lips. Depending on the player, the lips can make a dozen or so notes, and the piston valves create the rest.

Spring returns piston

Holes in valve

PISTONS UP

The column of vibrating air by-passes the piston valves.

THIRD PISTON DOWN

The longest side-section of tubing opens, lowering the note three semitones.

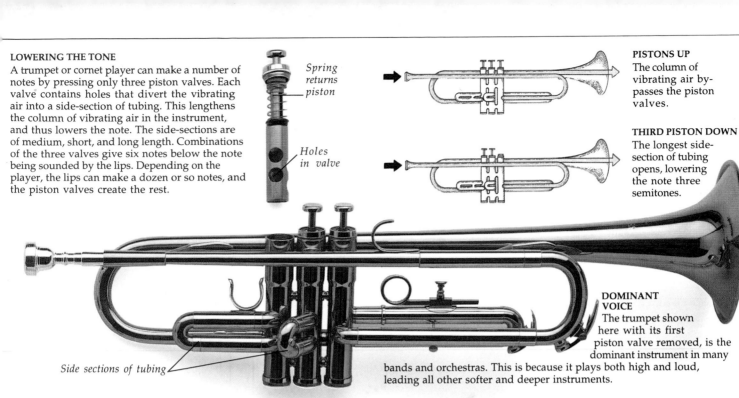

Side sections of tubing

DOMINANT VOICE

The trumpet shown here with its first piston valve removed, is the dominant instrument in many bands and orchestras. This is because it plays both high and loud, leading all other softer and deeper instruments.

"SATCHMO"

Louis Armstrong, nicknamed "Satchmo" because of his satchel-shaped mouth, revolutionized jazz in the 1920s with his brilliant trumpet playing. Until then jazz players had been mainly content to embellish tunes, with all the musicians playing together. Armstrong forged the first solo style in jazz by creating daring improvisations accompanied only by the rhythm secton.

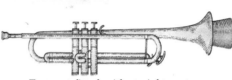

Trumpet fitted with straight mute

Straight mute   Cup mute   Harmon mute

MUTING THE SOUND

All brass instruments can be fitted with mutes that are pushed into, or over, the bell. Mutes reduce the volume of sound, but also greatly affect the tonal quality. A straight mute gives a thin, piercing sound, whereas a harmon mute produces the buzzy sound that is associated with the great jazz trumpet player, Miles Davis. Moving a mute in and out of the bell makes a "wha-wha" sound.

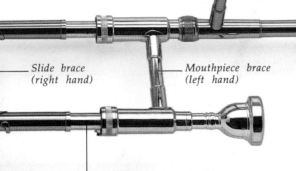

Wide, flared bell

BESSON

Slide brace (right hand)

Mouthpiece brace (left hand)

Inner tube of slide

LASTING DESIGN

The trombone is an instrument that has changed little over the years. Old paintings show that it reached its present form in the 15th century; only the bell has since altered, becoming wider over the last two centuries to give greater brilliance to the sound. The trombone has a slide to make the deeper notes, which are produced by the valves in other brass instruments. The player simply pushes out the slide to lengthen the tube. This has the advantage of enabling the player to "slide" from one note to the next, a characteristic feature of trombone music. A disadvantage is that the slide is cumbersome compared with valves, and the trombone is not suited to speedy playing. This instrument is the tenor trombone; a bass trombone has an extra section of tubing.

Curly horns and big tubas

A HOLLOW HORN was the ancestor of the horns that are now heard in orchestras and bands. The hollow sound of the horn - caused by the conical bore of the tube - means that it lacks the brilliance of the other principal brass instruments - the trumpet and trombone (pp. 22 - 23). Curly horns and a big tuba round out the sound of the brass section of a symphony orchestra, adding warmth and depth. The instruments require strong lips and lungs; the horn because it frequently has to produce high notes, the tuba because it is simply the most massive of all the wind instruments. In spite of the effort required to play these instruments, they can be played with great expression and sensitivity.

Rotary valves played by fingers of left hand

DUAL-NATIONALITY
The horn played in orchestras is often called the French horn, though in fact it developed mainly in Germany. This instrument is a double horn, and it is really two horns in one. The left thumb works a valve (p. 23) that switches between two sets of coiled tubing. One tube gives deep, warm notes, and the other gives high, bright notes. Straightened out, the double horn would be 9 m (30 ft) long!

The right hand fits inside the bell to adjust the notes

Wide flared bell supported by right hand

Wide conical bore gives mellow sound

Cup-shaped mouthpiece

BRED FROM THE BUGLE
This tenor horn is a descendant of the bugle, on which soldiers sound calls to duty. Valves were added to the bugle in the 19th century, notably by the famous Adolphe Sax, better known for the saxophone (pp. 14 - 15). A whole family of horns, usually called saxhorns, resulted.

Piston valve

ON PARADE
Military bands make much use of brass instruments, because they are easily carried on parade, and make a loud, stirring sound. Here a line of cornets precedes a row of French horns. Military bands also contain woodwind instruments, such as clarinets, and saxophones. Brass bands are normally limited to brass instruments, except for the bass drum that gives the beat.

HANDMADE HORNS
This 19th-century print of a horn factory in France shows the instruments being assembled. The horns were made in sections that were fitted together by hand.

LIGHT ON ITS FEET

The best-known piece of music for the tuba has the ungainly title *Tubby the Tuba*, which only adds to the tuba's undeserved reputation for clumping heavily around at the bottom of a brass band. In good hands the tuba can be nimble, and can produce a light and airy sound. The tuba is basically a huge, valved bugle held upright. It dates back to 1835, when it was invented in Germany as a bass instrument for military bands. Tubas come in a variety of sizes, ranging in pitch from deep to very deep. The largest tuba is a monster 2.4 m (8 ft) high, taller than the person playing it. If the tube from this tuba was uncoiled and stretched out, it would measure nearly 14 m (45 ft) long.

FORWARD, MARCH

This tuba is designed for playing with marching bands. The mouthpiece is bent round so the weight of the instrument can be supported on the shoulder. The bell points forward, sending the sound outward instead of upward.

AT EASE

The tuba is normally played sitting down with the instrument resting against the body. The tuba shown here has a fourth valve that extends its range of notes.

Large cup-shaped mouthpiece

Piston valves

Coils of tubing opened by piston valves

Modern brass instruments, like this tuba, keep their shine because they are sprayed with a chemical lacquer; once the instruments had to be polished to stop the metal tarnishing

SOUSA SOUND

The sousaphone is a deep-sounding instrument designed by the American bandmaster John Philip Sousa in 1898. It is placed over the shoulders with the bell raised high in the air. Lightweight models are made of fibreglass.

Breaking the silence

THE STUDY OF SOUND AND MUSIC began with notes plucked from a simple lyre in ancient Greece. Pythagoras (c. 582 - 507 B.C.), the famous scientist best known for squaring the hypotenuse, discovered that the pitch of a note created by a stretched string relates to the length of the string. If the lengths used are in simple proportions - such as 3 to 2, or 4 to 5 - then the notes which sound are in harmony. This principle lies behind all string instruments and, substituting air columns for strings, wind instruments (pp. 8 - 9).

Different notes can also be created by varying the tension and weight of the strings. The fingers of both hands make the sounds and create the notes in instruments like the violin, guitar and sitar. Being able to influence both pitch and tone so directly gives the players great power of musical expression. This sensitivity partly explains why the violin family plays such an important part in classical music; their bowed strings produce a wonderful soaring sound when played in large groups. The piano and harp are less direct in their action, but they compensate because they have many more strings that can be played to sound chords and create cascades of notes.

MUSICAL WEIGHT
The strings on string instruments have to be strong to stand up to high tension and vibration when being played. They are most commonly made of nylon thread or steel wire.

Soundboard is top
surface of hollow body

F-shaped soundholes
emit sound from
inside the body

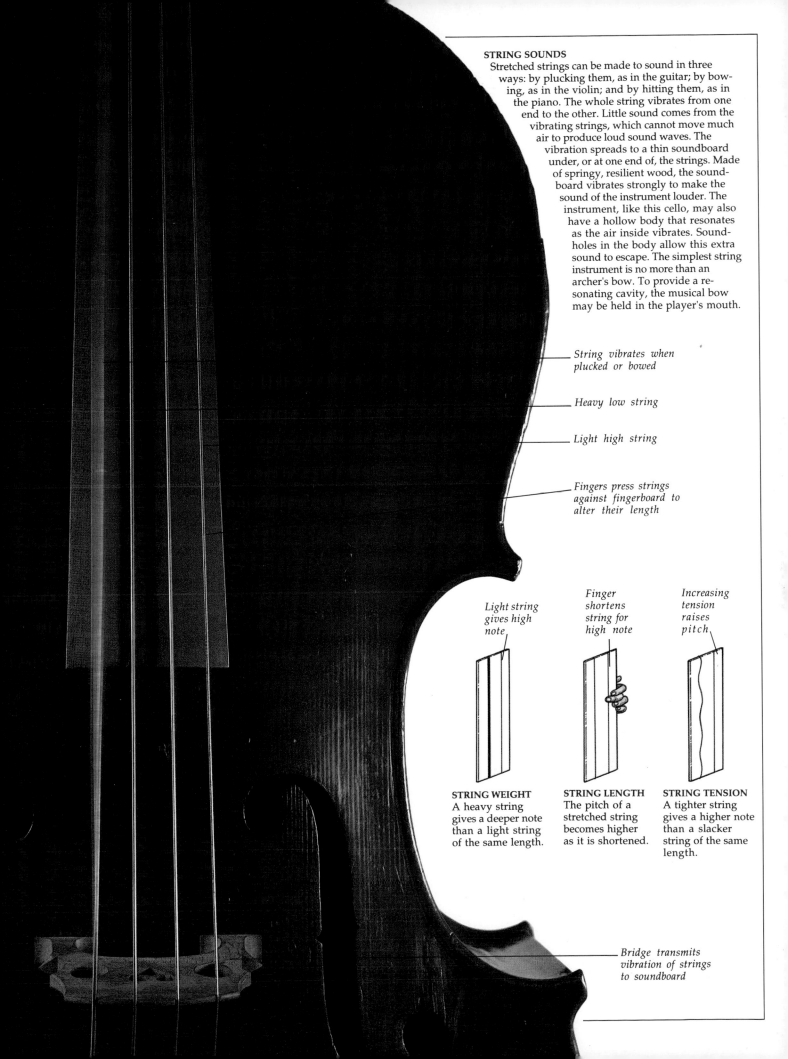

STRING SOUNDS

Stretched strings can be made to sound in three ways: by plucking them, as in the guitar; by bowing, as in the violin; and by hitting them, as in the piano. The whole string vibrates from one end to the other. Little sound comes from the vibrating strings, which cannot move much air to produce loud sound waves. The vibration spreads to a thin soundboard under, or at one end of, the strings. Made of springy, resilient wood, the soundboard vibrates strongly to make the sound of the instrument louder. The instrument, like this cello, may also have a hollow body that resonates as the air inside vibrates. Sound-holes in the body allow this extra sound to escape. The simplest string instrument is no more than an archer's bow. To provide a resonating cavity, the musical bow may be held in the player's mouth.

String vibrates when plucked or bowed

Heavy low string

Light high string

Fingers press strings against fingerboard to alter their length

Light string gives high note

Finger shortens string for high note

Increasing tension raises pitch

STRING WEIGHT
A heavy string gives a deeper note than a light string of the same length.

STRING LENGTH
The pitch of a stretched string becomes higher as it is shortened.

STRING TENSION
A tighter string gives a higher note than a slacker string of the same length.

Bridge transmits vibration of strings to soundboard

Early and unusual strings

Modern bowed string instruments are the culmination of many centuries of development. Their ancestors had a greater variety of features than modern standardized instruments, such as rounded or flat backs, fretted or fretless fingerboards, and varying numbers of strings including "sympathetic" strings. Playing techniques were different, with the smaller instruments being held vertically or against the chest instead of under the chin. Old features and techniques live on in folk instruments as well as revivals of ancient instruments.

A cathedral wood carving of an angel with a "viol", c. 1390

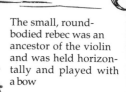

The small, round-bodied rebec was an ancestor of the violin and was held horizontally and played with a bow

Scroll with a carved lion's head

Ivory tuning peg

Plant-like patterns drawn in pen and ink

Carved head of a figure from mythology, possibly Ariadne; many instruments featured Cupid's head

Seven sympathetic strings lie beneath the seven melody strings

MIDDLE-EASTERN SPLENDOUR
The earliest bowed fiddles date back to the 10th century. This three-stringed spike fiddle was made in Iran in the 18th century. The spike extends from the ivory tuning pegs, passes through the neck and then pierces the round body. The instrument is made of wood with an intricate inlay.

HORSE PLAY
The *morin-khuur*, a Mongolian fiddle, has a square body and an elegant, carved horse's head on the scroll.

Vellum head of sound box

The spike passes right through the instrument

SCANDINAVIAN FOLK ART
This beautiful instrument is a folk fiddle of Norway. The decoration on the body is drawn in pen and ink, while the fingerboard is inlaid with bone and horn. Beneath the four strings that play melodies are four sympathetic strings. These are tuned to resonate (vibrate) as the melody strings sound. The fiddle became popular at Hardanger, Norway, in 1670 and this instrument dates from the mid 20th century.

The spike is rested on the ground for playing

CUPID'S INFLUENCE
Viola d'amore ("love-viol") seems a romantic name, but it refers to seven sympathetic strings that vibrate in sympathy with the seven melody strings. The strings and the shape of the body are similar to the viol but, like the viola (p.30), it is held under the chin and has no frets. Vivaldi wrote for the viola d'amore, but its delicate sound was of little value for orchestral use. This instrument was made in 1774.

Neck and scroll made of one piece of wood

THE DANCING MASTER
The kit (right) was played by a dancing master as he demonstrated steps to his pupils. The fiddle was small enough to fit into the pocket, hence in France the instrument was called a *pochette*, literally meaning "pocket". The bow could always be used, as shown in this late-18th-century engraving, to emphasize a point.

Miniature, carved head

FAMILY TRAITS
Viols are a family of six-stringed instruments that have frets like the guitar (p. 42) but are played with a bow. This fine bass viol was made in Britain in 1713. It has frets made of gut that can be moved to adjust the tuning.

Stroh violins had one string only

The amplifying horn can be turned to project the sound in the required direction

DANCING MINIATURE
The kit was a tiny fiddle that was popular during the 17th and 18th centuries. The round-bodied shape developed from the medieval rebec.

COUSIN OF THE CELLO
This 16th-century Italian painting shows a bass viol with some of the features of the cello (p. 31), which developed at this time. It has f-shaped soundholes, for example.

PLAYING THE VIOL
Viols were played with the hand under the bow, which gave a very even sound that blended well. The three largest viols - the treble, tenor and bass - were all played between the knees. They were popular until superseded by the violin family in the 18th century.

Metal amplifying horn

DESIGN CURIOSITY
The Stroh violin, or phonofiddle, was invented by the British musician Charles Stroh in 1901. Its single string caused a diaphragm at the side of the bridge to vibrate, and the horn amplified the sound made by the diaphragm in the same way as an early phonograph. It was used in variety and music hall acts. Amplifying horns were also added to the side of some ordinary fiddles for use in early recording studios.

C-shaped soundhole found on some members of the viol family

29

The violin family

THE VIOLIN achieved its present form in about 1550 and, together with the viola, cello and double bass, developed to virtual perfection over the next two centuries. Their rich and powerful sound, aided by playing techniques that gave greater expression, caused the violin family to supplant the viols and other bowed strings. With the foundation of the symphony orchestra and string quartet in the 18th century, the violin family established a dominant position in Western classical music. The violin also invaded folk music, and the double bass, jazz.

A DEVIL ON THE VIOLIN
The Italian violinist Niccolo Paganini (1782-1840) raised violin playing to incredible feats of virtuosity. He was reputed to have been in league with the devil, and to some people's ears his music has a demonic quality. Paganini is best known for his pieces for solo violin, one of which has been used as a theme for variations by several composers.

PRACTICE MAKES PERFECT
Made by an English violin-maker c. 1910, this peculiar-looking instrument was designed for violinists to practice on. Because it has no soundbox, when the strings are bowed or plucked they produce very little sound - ideal for playing in the middle of the night without disturbing the neighbours!

Bow's shape is the same for the violin, viola and cello

GENIUS AT WORK
The string instruments built by Stradivarius (c. 1644-1737) are said to be the finest ever made. The design has scarcely changed since then.

The thinnest string produces the highest notes

The string quartet (two violins, viola and cello), a classic combination of chamber music

VIOLIN
The violin is the smallest and highest-pitched member of the family and is played under the chin. The high E string has a brilliant sound that has attracted composers such as Bach and Mozart.

VIOLA
Although essentially the same shape as the violin, the viola is slightly bigger and is tuned below it and so produces a warm tenor sound. It is mainly used for inner parts in orchestras.

Violin

Viola

Cello

Double bass

Range of notes covered by the violin family compared to middle C

Each tuning
peg controls
one string

CELLO
The cello, or violon-
cello, is a low-pitched
instrument, its four
strings being tuned an
octave below the viola.
The cellist sits to play
it with the cello's body
resting on a metal
spike. It is an intensely
expressive instrument,
the high A string
having a wonderful
singing sound, and it is
often played solo.

The French bass
bow is held with
the fingers push-
ing down like a
violin or cello bow

The German bow has
a large frog (p. 33)
and is held with the
wrist upside-down
and the thumb press-
ing down on the bow

DOUBLE BASS
The deepest member of the string family is the double
bass. Measuring about 1.9m (6ft) from scroll to spike
this huge instrument rests on the floor with the
bass player standing behind. This double bass
has sloping shoulders like the bass viol
(p. 29), unlike other members of the
violin family. On some instruments a fifth string may be
added, When the double
bass is plucked, it
produces a deep, res-
onant sound. It is
played rhythmi-
cally in this
way in jazz
and folk
music.

F-shaped sound-
hole typical of
violin family

Frog

Spike on which cello
rests on ground

Making a violin

THE CREATION OF A GOOD VIOLIN is an exacting art, for the instrument is virtually made by hand. Materials must be carefully chosen and months of toil go into the shaping, finishing and assembly of the various parts. The end result is a beautiful instrument that is totally responsive to the player. The vibrations of the strings pass through the bridge into the hollow body. There they spread evenly and powerfully so that the body resonates to produce the rich, bright sound characteristic of the violin.

Violin-making methods have scarcely changed from the traditional skills used in this 18th-century workshop

Gouge

Thumb planes

Sections of maple for back

Belly ready for planing

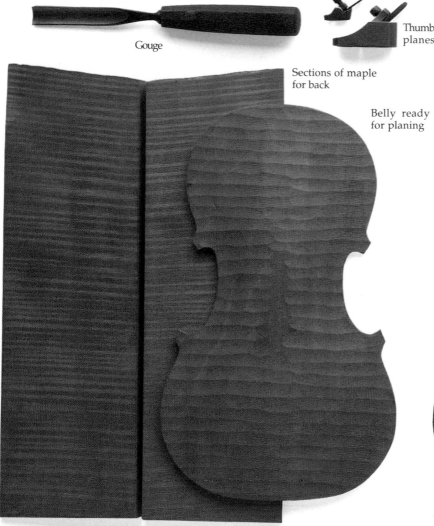

Purfling channel

Purfling made of mixed wood

CARVING THE BODY

A violin begins with sections of timber cut like slices of cake from a tree trunk. The wood must be both strong and springy to give the instrument a bright sound. A softwood such as pine or spruce is chosen for the front, or belly, of the body, and a hardwood, often maple, is used for the back. Each is usually formed of two sections glued together so that the grain runs evenly across it, although one piece backs and, more rarely, fronts are sometimes seen. The outline of the belly or back is then marked on the glued sections using a template and is carefully cut out with a fine saw. The wood is first carved into the approximate shape with a gouge. The violin maker then uses a succession of small planes to smoothe away the gouge marks - the tiniest plane is about the size of a thumbnail. Delicate work is required as even slight variations in the desired dimensions will alter the violin's sound. The centre of the plate is slightly rounded but the edges are flattened.

REFINING THE BODY

A special tool next cuts a narrow channel around the edge of the belly. A thin strip called the purfling is then inlaid into the channel. It is traditionally made of flexible layers of white maple and dyed pear wood. The purfling is decorative, but it also helps to prevent the wood splitting. The belly and back are then completed by carving the inside surface to shape. When finished, the belly has an even thickness of about 3 mm (.10 in), whereas the back is slightly thicker in the centre.

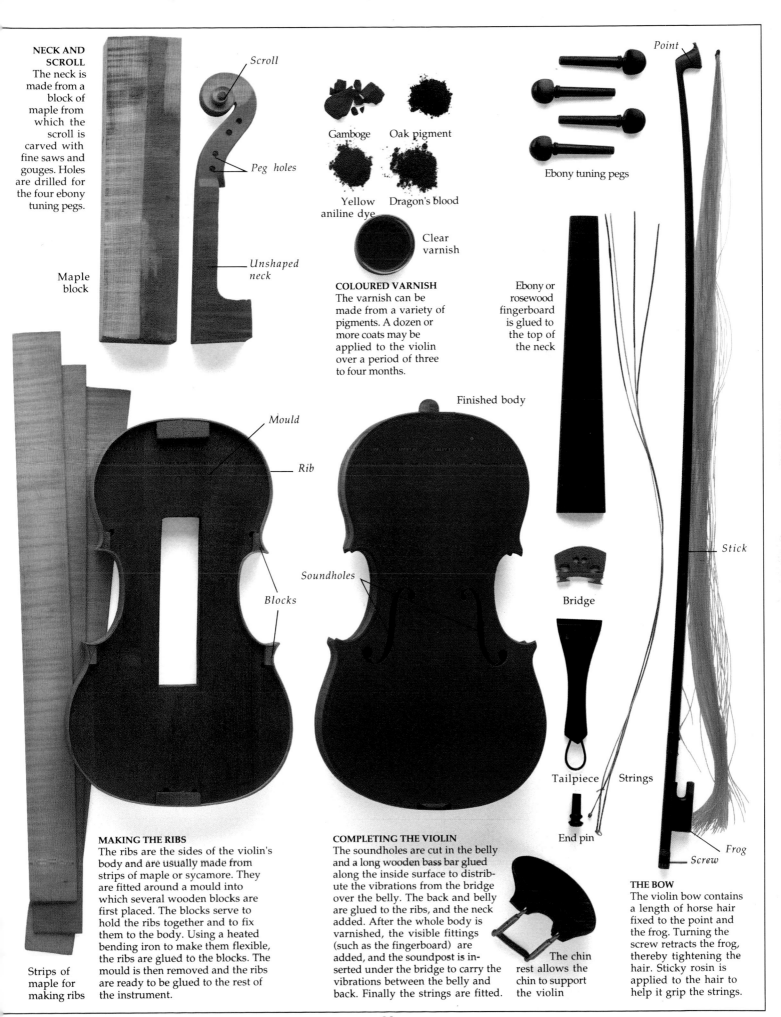

NECK AND SCROLL
The neck is made from a block of maple from which the scroll is carved with fine saws and gouges. Holes are drilled for the four ebony tuning pegs.

Scroll

Peg holes

Unshaped neck

Maple block

Strips of maple for making ribs

Mould

Rib

Soundholes

Blocks

Gamboge

Oak pigment

Yellow aniline dye

Dragon's blood

Clear varnish

COLOURED VARNISH
The varnish can be made from a variety of pigments. A dozen or more coats may be applied to the violin over a period of three to four months.

Finished body

Point

Ebony tuning pegs

Ebony or rosewood fingerboard is glued to the top of the neck

Stick

Bridge

Tailpiece

Strings

End pin

Frog

Screw

MAKING THE RIBS
The ribs are the sides of the violin's body and are usually made from strips of maple or sycamore. They are fitted around a mould into which several wooden blocks are first placed. The blocks serve to hold the ribs together and to fix them to the body. Using a heated bending iron to make them flexible, the ribs are glued to the blocks. The mould is then removed and the ribs are ready to be glued to the rest of the instrument.

COMPLETING THE VIOLIN
The soundholes are cut in the belly and a long wooden bass bar glued along the inside surface to distribute the vibrations from the bridge over the belly. The back and belly are glued to the ribs, and the neck added. After the whole body is varnished, the visible fittings (such as the fingerboard) are added, and the soundpost is inserted under the bridge to carry the vibrations between the belly and back. Finally the strings are fitted.

The chin rest allows the chin to support the violin

THE BOW
The violin bow contains a length of horse hair fixed to the point and the frog. Turning the screw retracts the frog, thereby tightening the hair. Sticky rosin is applied to the hair to help it grip the strings.

Harps and lyres

HARPS AND LYRES are strongly associated with goodness: angels traditionally carry harps and the connection goes far back to the legend of Orpheus, who charmed all with his lyre. The instruments are in fact of ancient origin, and they appear all over the world. They consist basically of strings that stretch over a frame, and may have descended from the archer's bow. Harps and lyres are usually plucked, but bowed lyres such as the Swedish *tallharpa* survive in Scandinavia. The strings can each sound a different note and are often tuned to a scale of notes. The elegant concert harp, from which angelic music seems to emerge effortlessly, is something of a beast to play - as well as having 47 strings to pluck, there are seven pedals that make different notes.

MAGICAL CHARM
This 3rd-century mosaic from Tarsus in Turkey portrays Orpheus charming the beasts with his lyre. The Greek myth tells how Orpheus' playing so delighted the king of the underworld that he was allowed to bring his wife Eurydice back from the dead provided he did not gaze on her until they reached the upper world. But Orpheus could not resist stealing a look and lost Eurydice.

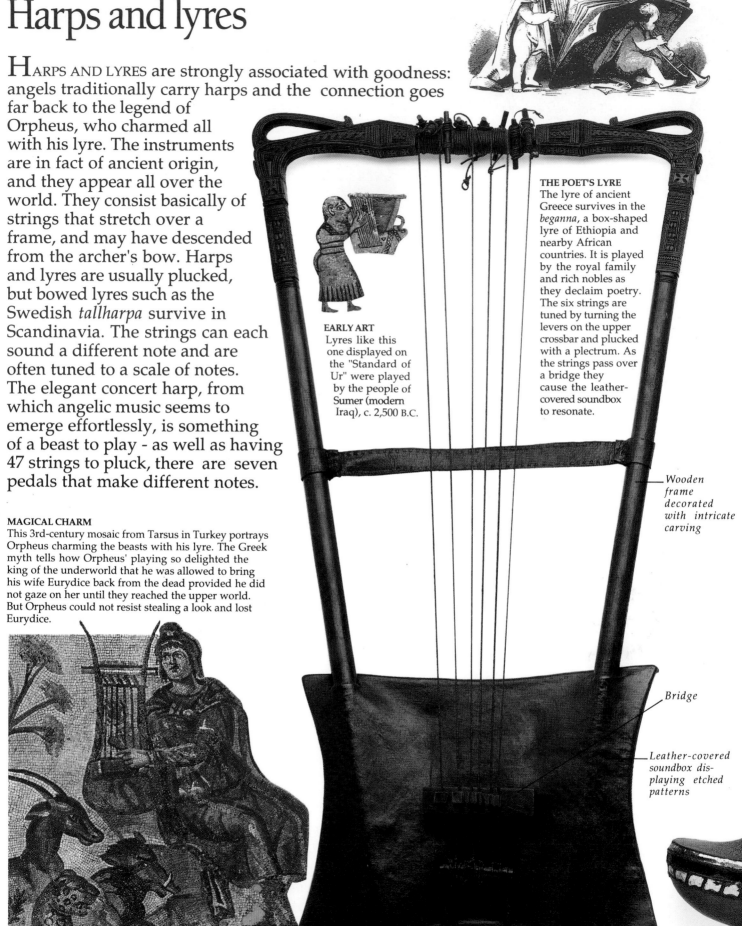

EARLY ART
Lyres like this one displayed on the "Standard of Ur" were played by the people of Sumer (modern Iraq), c. 2,500 B.C.

THE POET'S LYRE
The lyre of ancient Greece survives in the *beganna*, a box-shaped lyre of Ethiopia and nearby African countries. It is played by the royal family and rich nobles as they declaim poetry. The six strings are tuned by turning the levers on the upper crossbar and plucked with a plectrum. As the strings pass over a bridge they cause the leather-covered soundbox to resonate.

Wooden frame decorated with intricate carving

Bridge

Leather-covered soundbox displaying etched patterns

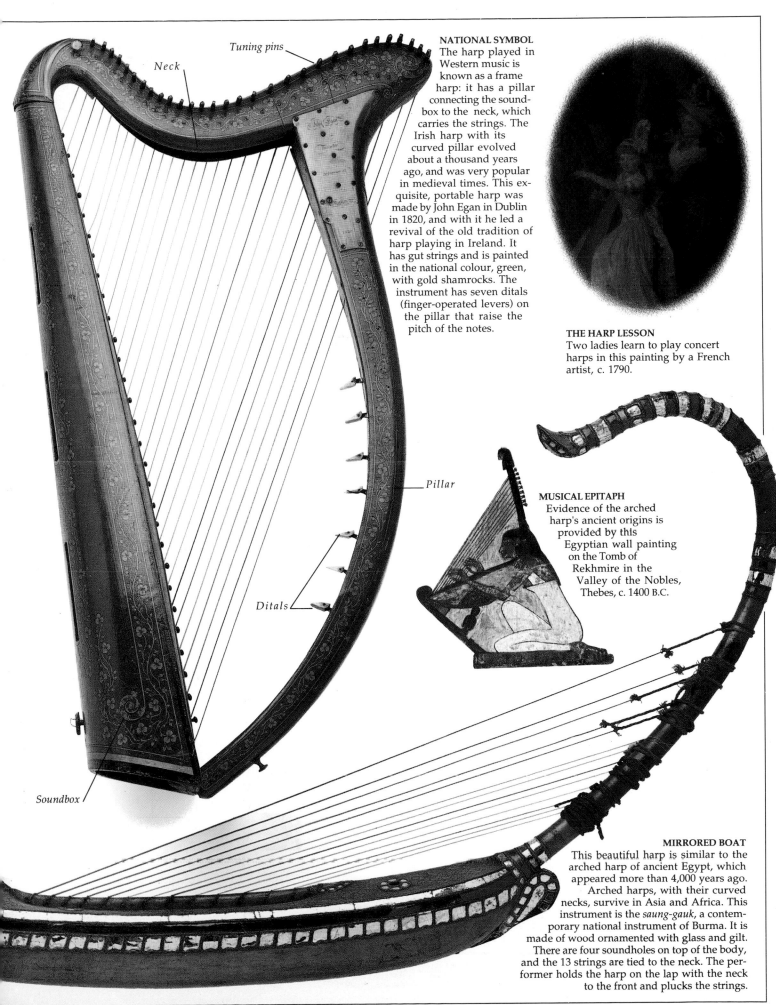

Tuning pins

Neck

NATIONAL SYMBOL
The harp played in Western music is known as a frame harp: it has a pillar connecting the sound-box to the neck, which carries the strings. The Irish harp with its curved pillar evolved about a thousand years ago, and was very popular in medieval times. This exquisite, portable harp was made by John Egan in Dublin in 1820, and with it he led a revival of the old tradition of harp playing in Ireland. It has gut strings and is painted in the national colour, green, with gold shamrocks. The instrument has seven ditals (finger-operated levers) on the pillar that raise the pitch of the notes.

THE HARP LESSON
Two ladies learn to play concert harps in this painting by a French artist, c. 1790.

Pillar

MUSICAL EPITAPH
Evidence of the arched harp's ancient origins is provided by this Egyptian wall painting on the Tomb of Rekhmire in the Valley of the Nobles, Thebes, c. 1400 B.C.

Ditals

Soundbox

MIRRORED BOAT
This beautiful harp is similar to the arched harp of ancient Egypt, which appeared more than 4,000 years ago. Arched harps, with their curved necks, survive in Asia and Africa. This instrument is the *saung-gauk*, a contemporary national instrument of Burma. It is made of wood ornamented with glass and gilt. There are four soundholes on top of the body, and the 13 strings are tied to the neck. The performer holds the harp on the lap with the neck to the front and plucks the strings.

From pears to whole fishes

DATING BACK SOME 4,000 YEARS, the lute is the oldest ancestor of the violin and guitar. Like the guitar, the lute is plucked, and usually has frets. It can be distinguished from the guitar by its characteristic, half-pear-shaped body. Old lutes are recognizable because they often have a bewildering array of strings - some have as many as 13 pairs. Placing four fingers over them can be a struggle, and the lutenist probably spends more time tuning the instrument than playing it. This was one of the reasons why the lute fell from favour in Western music some two centuries ago.

17th-century musician with a *colascione*

SOLO ARMADILLO
The *Charango* is a small South Armerican lute, the back of which is made from the carapace (horny skin) of an armadillo. This instrument was made in Bolivia and has five pairs of strings. The armadillo is now protected, so most modern *charangoes* have wooden backs.

Classic round-backed lute of the 15th century

ARAB ANCESTOR
The classical lute evolved from the *'ud* , an Arab lute that reached Europe in the 13th century. This Moroccan *'ud* is only about 40 years old. It has an S-shaped peg-box, and a deeper body and narrower neck than the classic lute, popular in Europe in the 15th and 16th centuries.

BENT OVER BACKWARDS
Lute pegboxes bend back at a slight or steep angle. They may also have pairs of strings instead of single strings.

The armadillo carapace was dried in a mould to give it the right shape

Six-banded armadillo

Five pairs of open strings

Six pairs of strings and two single strings

HIGHLY STRUNG
This German baroque lute was made by Johann Christian Hoffmann, a friend of J.S. Bach, in the 18th century. It is a particular type of bass lute with two pegboxes. This one has 14 strings, stopped by the fingers on the unfretted fingerboard, and 10 open bass strings. It was used to play a continuo (bass line and chords) in the baroque music of the time.

Singing was often accompanied by a lute

Separate pegbox for open strings

Pegbox for fingered strings

FISH-FINGERED
Lutes played in folk music, like this unusual fish-shaped instrument, often lack the deep bowl of the classic lute. This is a *rajao,* a Portuguese lute with five single strings. It comes from Madeira, and was made in the 19th century.

STRUNG ALONG
A Mongolian woman dressed in traditional costume plays the *san xian,* which is a Chinese lute similar to the Japanese *shamisen.* The lute's name means "three strings".

Five tuning pegs in the "tail"

Fretted fingerboard

Tuning peg

Heart-shaped soundhole

SOVIET SOUNDS
The Russian *balalaika* has a tri-angular body with a flat back and three strings. Here the pegbox is carved to form two horses' heads. Other folk-music lutes include the mandolin from Italy and the Greek *bouzouki.* The musicians often play a melody by repeatedly strumming one string with a plectrum.

Three strings of silk or nylon

Fish-shaped body lacks the deep bowl of the classic lute

Three strings

Ribs of sandal-wood, mulberry or quince

Catskin belly and back

Bone plectrum

STICKING ITS NECK OUT
The *shamisen* is a long-necked lute that is much played in Japan, for example in the *kabuki* theatre, where it provides the music for the traditional plays. The three strings have various tunings, including one for comic music. The player uses a bone plectrum called a *bachi* to strike both the strings and the catskin belly of the *shamisen.* The belly is strengthened with parchment to withstand the regular battering it receives.

TEA-TIME IN JAPAN
Here the Japanese tea ceremony is accompanied by music from two lutes - the *shamisen* (left) and short-necked *biwa* (centre). The *biwa* developed from the Chinese *pipa,* introduced to Japan a thousand years ago.

37

From gourd to board

Little material is required to make the ground zither of Africa and south-east Asia: dig a small pit in the ground and stretch a string across it; twang the string and the air in the pit resonates with a note. This principle links all zithers that have strings stretched across a soundbox - plucking or beating the strings makes the soundbox re-sound with music. Zithers are popular in folk music, and in China the *qin* zither once held a privileged status, and inspired philosophical theories. Zithers are quite easy to play because you can make a tune simply by plucking the strings. Use two hands with a large set of strings, and a melody and accompaniment are possible. A fingerboard and frets enable a few melody strings to play a tune, while separate open strings provide the accompaniment.

Strips vibrate between bridges

Cane bridge

Hollow gourd resonates

STRIPS FOR STRINGS
In this raft zither from Nigeria, the strings are thin strips of cane cut from the body of the bamboo "raft".

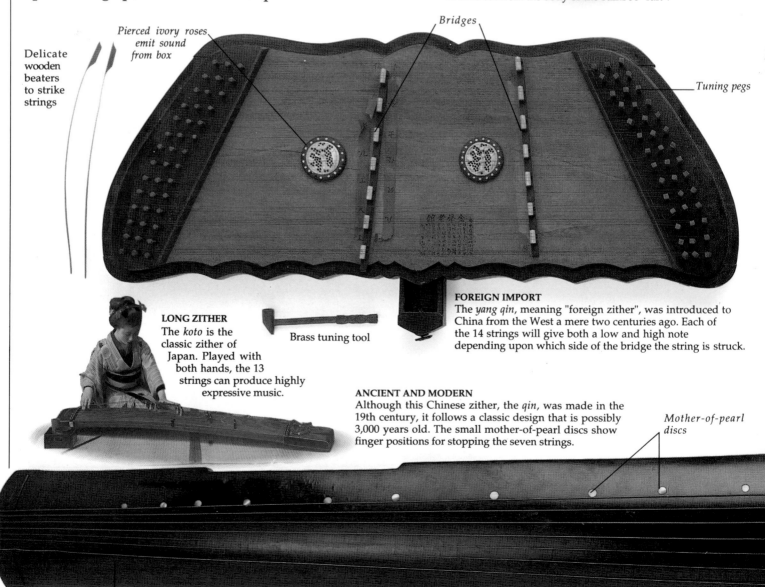

Pierced ivory roses emit sound from box

Bridges

Delicate wooden beaters to strike strings

Tuning pegs

Brass tuning tool

LONG ZITHER
The *koto* is the classic zither of Japan. Played with both hands, the 13 strings can produce highly expressive music.

FOREIGN IMPORT
The *yang qin*, meaning "foreign zither", was introduced to China from the West a mere two centuries ago. Each of the 14 strings will give both a low and high note depending upon which side of the bridge the string is struck.

ANCIENT AND MODERN
Although this Chinese zither, the *qin*, was made in the 19th century, it follows a classic design that is possibly 3,000 years old. The small mother-of-pearl discs show finger positions for stopping the seven strings.

Mother-of-pearl discs

Board lacquered in tortoise-shell pattern

MUSICAL STICK
The principles that produce music from all hand-held string instruments can be seen in this *tzeze*, a simple stick zither from Uganda. A string is fixed to each end of the stick. Plucking with one hand sounds the string, which vibrates to make the gourd resonate. Pressing the fingers of the other hand against the frets shortens the string and varies the pitch of note being sounded.

SHAPELY PSALTERY
The psaltery was a medieval zither. It was sometimes made in unusual shapes - some were even shaped like a pig's head - with strings of different lengths. The psaltery developed from the *qanum*, a zither from the Middle East that reached Europe in the 11th century.

LUTE-LIKE ZITHER
The *bandura*, a traditional instrument of the Ukraine, combines features of the zither and the lute (p. 36). It has melody strings stopped by the fingers on the double fingerboard, while the open strings are plucked to accompany the melody. This instrument, made in c. 1945, is intricately decorated with inlays and carved oak leaves.

Inserted pieces of wood

Frets

Strings plucked by fingers

Double fingerboard

Hollow gourd

Stick

Inlay of zither player

Melody strings

Open strings

TWANGING TUBE
The island of Madagascar, off the southeast coast of Africa, is the home of this simple tube zither, the *valiha*. The zither is made from a piece of bamboo out of which strings have been cut and left attached at both ends. In order to allow the strings to vibrate, small pieces of wood have been inserted underneath. The player holds the tube upright, or under the arm, and plucks the taut strings with the fingers. Tube zithers can also be found in southeast Asia.

Mother-of-pearl inlay

Carved oak-leaf decoration

Indian strings

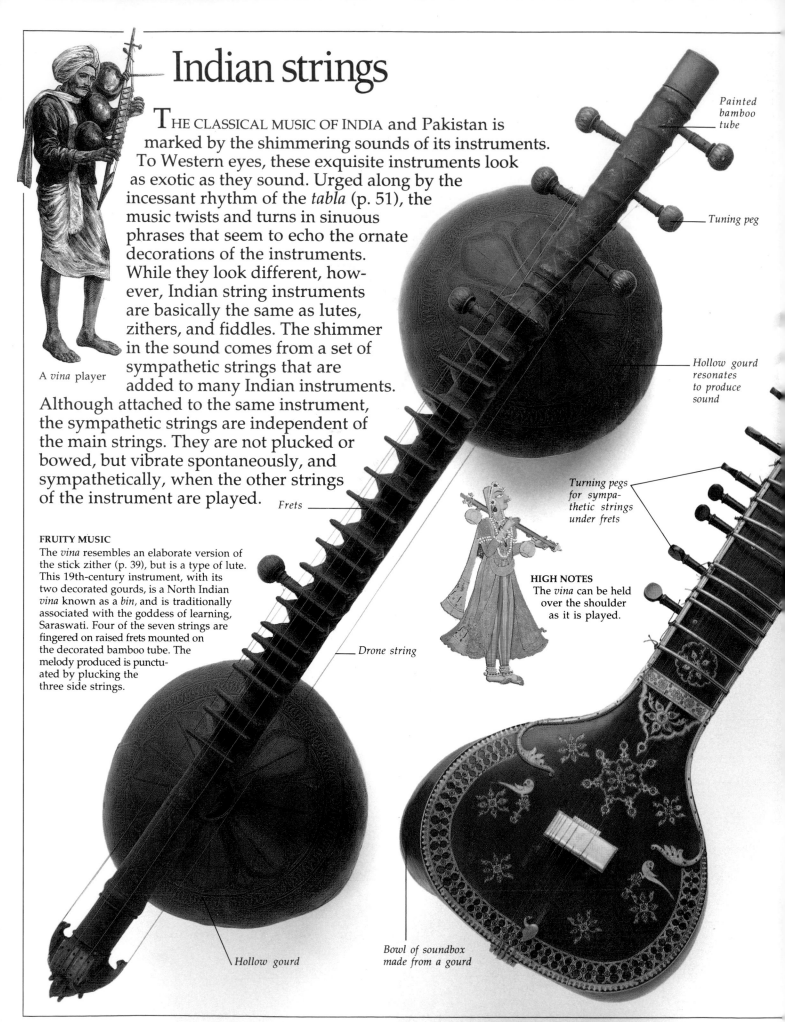

THE CLASSICAL MUSIC OF INDIA and Pakistan is marked by the shimmering sounds of its instruments. To Western eyes, these exquisite instruments look as exotic as they sound. Urged along by the incessant rhythm of the *tabla* (p. 51), the music twists and turns in sinuous phrases that seem to echo the ornate decorations of the instruments. While they look different, however, Indian string instruments are basically the same as lutes, zithers, and fiddles. The shimmer in the sound comes from a set of sympathetic strings that are added to many Indian instruments. Although attached to the same instrument, the sympathetic strings are independent of the main strings. They are not plucked or bowed, but vibrate spontaneously, and sympathetically, when the other strings of the instrument are played.

A *vina* player

Painted bamboo tube

Tuning peg

Hollow gourd resonates to produce sound

Turning pegs for sympathetic strings under frets

Frets

HIGH NOTES
The *vina* can be held over the shoulder as it is played.

FRUITY MUSIC
The *vina* resembles an elaborate version of the stick zither (p. 39), but is a type of lute. This 19th-century instrument, with its two decorated gourds, is a North Indian *vina* known as a *bin*, and is traditionally associated with the goddess of learning, Saraswati. Four of the seven strings are fingered on raised frets mounted on the decorated bamboo tube. The melody produced is punctuated by plucking the three side strings.

Drone string

Hollow gourd

Bowl of soundbox made from a gourd

BIRD SONG
A type of long lute, this 20th-century *sitar* has seven main strings that pass over arched metal frets. These frets allow the player to pull the strings and bend the notes to produce the *sitar's* sinuous sound.

THE SOUND OF INDIA
Popularized in the West by Ravi Shankar and other famous Indian musicians, the *sitar* has become the best-known of all Indian instruments. As a result, the figure of the *sitar* player, seated on the floor to play, is a familiar sight.

Wooden tuning pegs

UNDERCURRENTS
Like the *sitar*, which it accompanies in classical Indian music, the *tambura* is a long lute. Beneath the *sitar's* swirling flow of melody, the *tambura* plays a steady drone. The painted figures represent Rama and his wife Sita, the subjects of an ancient Hindu epic poem.

Tuning pegs run along the length of the neck

PROUD AS A PEACOCK
This instrument is a dilruba, a magnificent instrument that is played with a bow. It has the body of a sarangi but the neck and strings are like a sitar. The soundbox is shaped like a peacock. It is also called the mayuri or ta'us - both words meaning "peacock". Peacock sitars like this one, contributed to the splendour of the courts of the Indian princes.

This musician plays a fiddle similar to a *sarangi*

Ivory bridge

Peacock feathers decorate the instrument

Waisted body made from a single block of wood

To replace strings, the neck of the peacock can be hinged down

Ornate soundbox

WASTING AWAY
The Indian form of the fiddle is the *sarangi*. The chunky body is held upright and played with a bow. Sympathetic strings pass through the holes in the wide fingerboard.

41

Creating a guitar

THE ACOUSTIC GUITAR IS FOREVER LINKED with Spain, so much so that it is often called the Spanish guitar. Flamenco, the folk music of Spain, is renowned for its exciting guitar music as well as its energetic dancing. The instrument, with its body shaped like a figure eight, probably came to Spain from North Africa, and may be descended from lutes like the '*ud* (p. 36). By the 17th century, the guitar was being played all over Europe. Today acoustic and electric guitars (pp. 58 - 59) have spread throughout the world, and dominate popular music and much folk music in America and Europe.

This portrayal of a 19th-century Spanish guitar player shows the instrument in its present form.

Top block joins the neck to the body

CLASSICAL GUITAR
This is the traditional form of the guitar, also known as the Spanish guitar. It has six strings, usually made of nylon, and a wide neck. The design dates back to the mid-19th century, when it was perfected by a Spanish carpenter called Antonio de Torres Jurado, often known simply as Torres. Guitars played in popular music usually have a fingerplate fixed to the body to protect it.

Soundboard with struts for strength

Mould

Wooden linings are glued along top and bottom edges of ribs

MAKING THE SOUNDBOARD
The most important part of the guitar is the soundboard - the upper part of the body underneath the strings. It is made of two pieces of pine, spruce, cedar, or redwood that are glued together and then cut and shaped, or it may be made from layers of plywood. To strengthen the soundboard, struts are glued across the inside in a pattern that is crucial to the tone of the guitar. The sides, or ribs, of the guitar are made of two strips of rosewood, walnut, mahogany, maple, or sycamore. The strips are heated and shaped in a mould. Wooden blocks and linings are fixed to the inside of the ribs to make good joints for the soundboard and other parts.

Flat-top guitar with fingerplate

Classical guitar

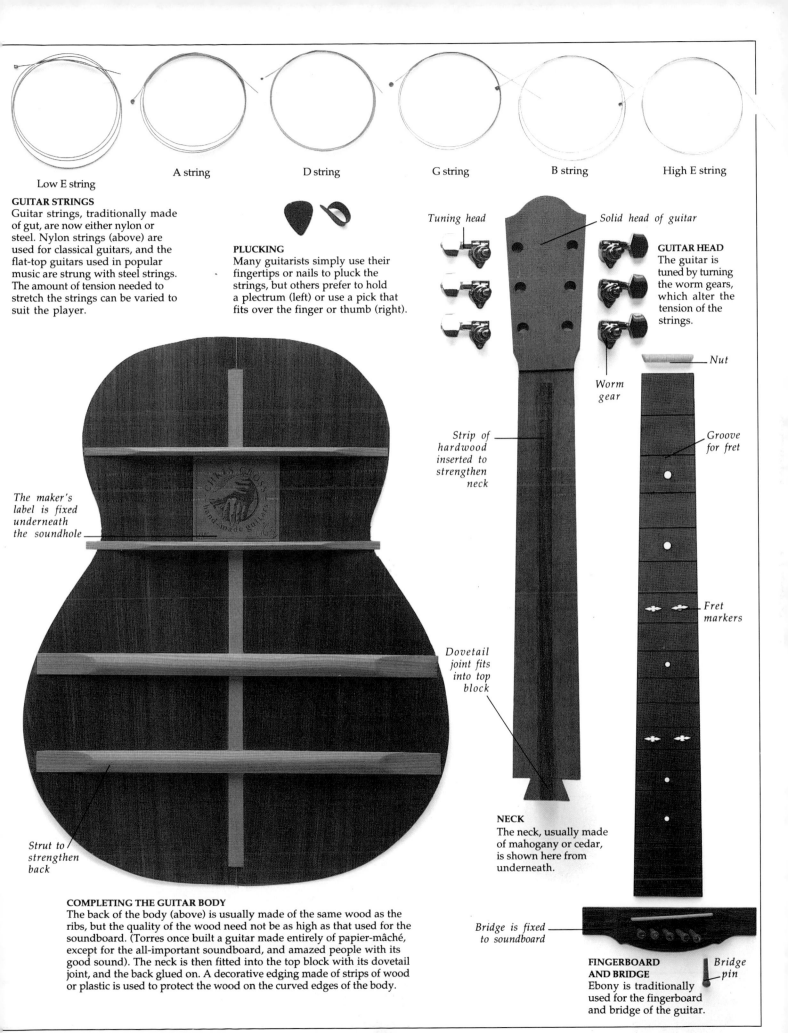

Low E string   A string   D string   G string   B string   High E string

GUITAR STRINGS
Guitar strings, traditionally made of gut, are now either nylon or steel. Nylon strings (above) are used for classical guitars, and the flat-top guitars used in popular music are strung with steel strings. The amount of tension needed to stretch the strings can be varied to suit the player.

PLUCKING
Many guitarists simply use their fingertips or nails to pluck the strings, but others prefer to hold a plectrum (left) or use a pick that fits over the finger or thumb (right).

Tuning head

Solid head of guitar

GUITAR HEAD
The guitar is tuned by turning the worm gears, which alter the tension of the strings.

Worm gear

Nut

Strip of hardwood inserted to strengthen neck

Groove for fret

The maker's label is fixed underneath the soundhole

Fret markers

Dovetail joint fits into top block

NECK
The neck, usually made of mahogany or cedar, is shown here from underneath.

Strut to strengthen back

COMPLETING THE GUITAR BODY
The back of the body (above) is usually made of the same wood as the ribs, but the quality of the wood need not be as high as that used for the soundboard. (Torres once built a guitar made entirely of papier-mâché, except for the all-important soundboard, and amazed people with its good sound). The neck is then fitted into the top block with its dovetail joint, and the back glued on. A decorative edging made of strips of wood or plastic is used to protect the wood on the curved edges of the body.

Bridge is fixed to soundboard

FINGERBOARD AND BRIDGE
Ebony is traditionally used for the fingerboard and bridge of the guitar.

Bridge pin

Keynotes

MASTERING NUMEROUS STRINGS, like those of the zither (p 38), can be a problem. The solution to tattered and tangled fingers came with the addition of a keyboard in the 15th century. Keyboards had been used to sound sets of pipes in organs (p. 18) for centuries. But using them to sound strings led to the development of domestic instruments with greater powers of expression. In the spinet, virginal, and the larger harpsichord, the keys worked a mechanism to pluck the strings. Their restricted range of volume, however, led to the invention of the piano, a keyboard instrument that hammered the strings to play both soft and loud or, in Italian, *piano* and *forte*.

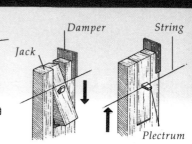

PAINTED VIRGINAL
This 17th-century painting by the Dutch artist Vermeer shows a young girl seated at the keyboard of a virginal. The lid of her beautifully decorated instrument is lifted to reveal a painted landscape. The shape of the case means that the strings of this virginal run almost parallel to the keyboard.

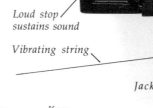

Loud stop sustains sound

Vibrating string

Key

Jack

KEY PRESSED
Pressing the key of a spinet, virginal, or harpsichord, raises a wooden jack with a quill or plectrum that plucks the string.

Damper

String

Jack

Plectrum

KEY RETURNS
The plectrum pivots away from the string as the damper falls.

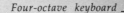

Four-octave keyboard

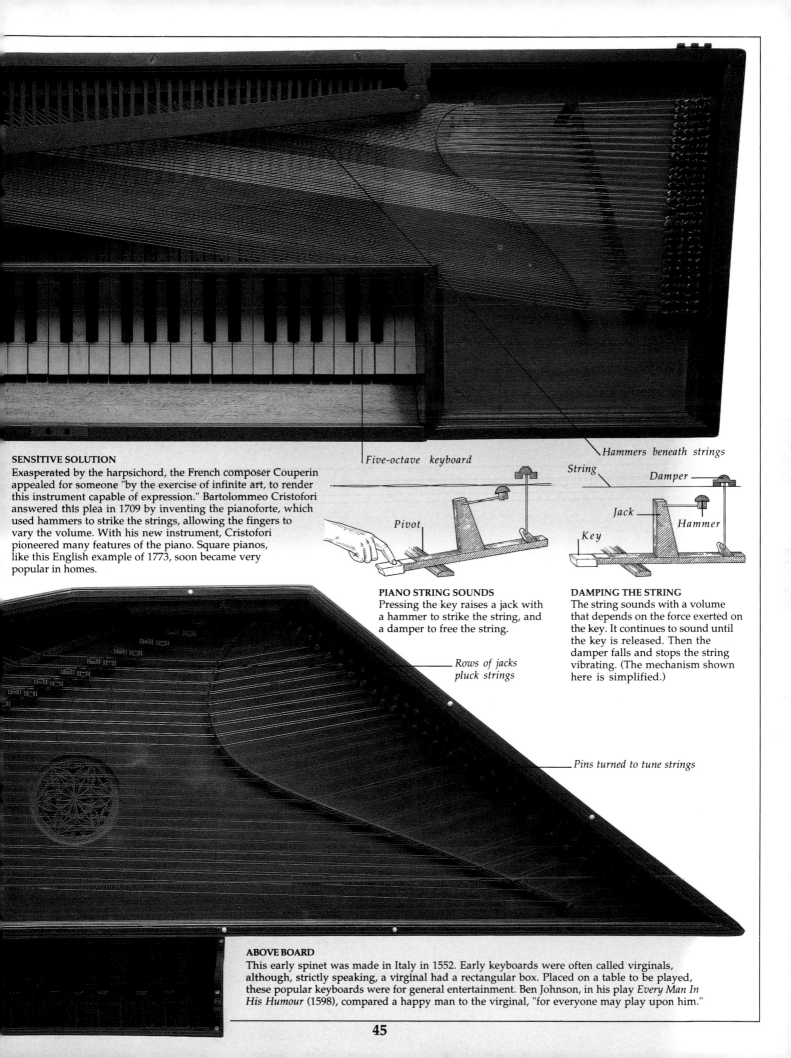

SENSITIVE SOLUTION
Exasperated by the harpsichord, the French composer Couperin appealed for someone "by the exercise of infinite art, to render this instrument capable of expression." Bartolommeo Cristofori answered this plea in 1709 by inventing the pianoforte, which used hammers to strike the strings, allowing the fingers to vary the volume. With his new instrument, Cristofori pioneered many features of the piano. Square pianos, like this English example of 1773, soon became very popular in homes.

Five-octave keyboard

Hammers beneath strings

String   *Damper*

Jack

Pivot   *Hammer*

Key

PIANO STRING SOUNDS
Pressing the key raises a jack with a hammer to strike the string, and a damper to free the string.

Rows of jacks pluck strings

DAMPING THE STRING
The string sounds with a volume that depends on the force exerted on the key. It continues to sound until the key is released. Then the damper falls and stops the string vibrating. (The mechanism shown here is simplified.)

Pins turned to tune strings

ABOVE BOARD
This early spinet was made in Italy in 1552. Early keyboards were often called virginals, although, strictly speaking, a virginal had a rectangular box. Placed on a table to be played, these popular keyboards were for general entertainment. Ben Johnson, in his play *Every Man In His Humour* (1598), compared a happy man to the virginal, "for everyone may play upon him."

Grand and upright

No OTHER SOLO INSTRUMENT has the power of the piano, which can respond so readily to the touch of the fingers. The ability to play a different note with each finger, and to make each note soft or loud gives the piano a tremendous range of expression. A pianist can produce magnificent music either alone or with the accompaniment of an orchestra. The piano is also important in popular music and jazz, where it can dominate or support other instruments. The best pianos are grand pianos, and they are "grand" in both size and sound. Upright pianos are more common because they take up less floor space and are less expensive. A good upright piano should maintain the full and bright sound of the grand piano, despite its size and shape.

The composer and virtuoso pianist Franz Liszt in 1824

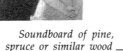

PIANO IN THE PARLOUR
The piano was more popular a century ago, before the gramophone and radio brought music into the home. People would gather around the piano for a sing-song, and guest houses advertised the presence of a piano as motels now advertise colour television.

CASE HISTORY
This grand piano of 1878 is typically ornate, but its overall shape has not changed since the piano was invented in 1709. The case is shaped to contain the long brass strings, and curves in for the shorter treble strings.

Bass notes have thick single strings about the same length as the medium strings

Wooden case

Soundboard of pine, spruce or similar wood

Treble notes each have three strings to make them sound louder

HIGH TENSION
All pianos contain an iron frame on which the metal strings are stretched with great force. Pressing the keys makes felt-tipped hammers strike the strings, which vibrate. This causes the soundboard underneath the strings to resonate, making the piano's distinctive sound.

88-note keyboard

Piano action involves
a complex system of
levers to work the
hammers and dampers

Felt-tipped hammers

Tuning pins

HUPFELD

Soft pedal raises
a lever to move
hammers nearer
to the strings

Sustaining or
"loud" pedal
raises dampers
from strings to
sustain sound

Medium notes have
double strings

The strings pull on the
iron frame with a total
force of about 18 tonnes

Musical impact

MUSIC HAS TO BE COAXED from many instruments: a violin must be fingered with dexterity, a flute blown with sensitivity. Few such requirements apparently apply to percussion instruments. Just hit them, shake them, or scrape them and out come the sounds. But playing percussion is not quite so simple. Exactly the right amount of force must be used to set the instrument vibrating in the right way. The stretched skin in the head of a drum has to vibrate to set the air inside ringing with sound. A smaller or tighter head makes a higher note, following the same principle as a stretched string (pp. 26 - 27). Orchestral timpani or kettle drums are tuned to certain notes in this way. In other percussion instruments, the whole body of the instrument may vibrate to give out sound, for example cymbals and rattles. Tuned percussion instruments like the xylophone make definite notes, in which bars or bells of different sizes are struck to ring out the notes.

RIPPLES OF SOUND
Percussion instruments vibrate to make sounds. When an instrument's surface is struck it vibrates, often in a complex pattern that is difficult to measure. The set of images shown here has been produced by a powerful computer to show the pattern of vibrations through a stretched skin, such as the head of a drum. The whole sequence would take place in a fraction of a second. Green shows the initial level of the skin. Blue indicates parts of the skin that are below this level, and red shows the parts that are above. In the first picture the centre of the skin is being struck. A wave spreads out in a circle, like the ripple created by dropping a stone into a pool of water. This wave then reflects from the sides of the skin, where they are clamped to the edge of the drum, setting up vibration patterns. The patterns become increasingly complex as the curved waves cross each other, and then reflect from the sides again.

1

2

3

4

5

6

7

8

The edges of the cymbal vibrate so fast that they make a blur

GOOD VIBRATIONS
A cymbal is the thin disc of
bronze held at the centre, so that the
edges are free to vibrate. Striking the cymbal
with a stick makes it sound with a loud crash.
The impact causes the metal disc to distort slightly, but because it is flexible, it immediately snaps back and sets the whole disc flexing to and fro,
in a similar way to a drum skin (left). It takes some time for these
vibrations to die out. Striking the cymbal in different places varies the
sound, because different kinds of vibration patterns are set up.

*Thin bronze disc
clamped at the centre*

Rhythm and ritual

African drum suspended from neck

APART FROM the physical effort that goes into beating a drum, the music often gathers its own energy as strong rhythms seem to drive it forward. A vitality is created that sets bodies swaying, hands clapping, and feet tapping. Shaking rattles and scraping instruments often help to whip up the energy of the music. Music, however, is not the sole purpose of these instruments. Drums and rattles have always played an important part in rituals, and "talking" drums can even send messages far afield.

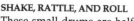

SHAKE, RATTLE, AND ROLL
These small drums are half-drum and half-rattle. Twirling the handle vigorously causes the beads on the cords to fly to and fro and strike the drum heads with a rattling sound. Glass beads may be used, pellets of wax or just knots in the cords. The Chinese *t'ao-ku* with its five drums dates back around 3,000 years. The other instrument is from India. Rattle drums, also called clapper drums or pellet drums, are common in Asia. They are used as toys or by street vendors to attract attention.

Indian rattle drum

Chinese rattle drum

Young boy playing a pair of African conical drums

Wooden body inlaid with tortoise-shell and mother-of-pearl

The skin is struck with the fingers or a curved stick

Pressing the cords increases the tension of the skins in the two heads and raises the notes

MARCHING DRUM
Military bands contain many drums that play a constant rhythm to which the soldiers can march in step. The drums are carried on a sling round the body so that the drummer can walk.

DANCE RHYTHM
The *tabor* was the most common drum in medieval Europe, and was often used to lead the dancing. The musician would beat on the drum with a stick held in one hand, while playing a pipe held in the other hand.

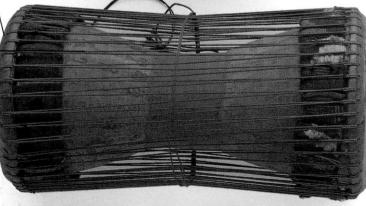

DRINKING DRUM
Goblet drums, single-headed drums in the shape of a goblet, are popular in Arab countries. This example is an Egyptian *darabuka*. The "goblet" is made of pottery or wood. The drum is struck at the centre and edges of the skin with two hands.

BEATING WORDS
This *kalengo* from Nigeria is renowned for its ability to "talk". By pressing the cords on this waisted drum, the drummer can raise and lower the note produced. The drum makes the sound of a tonal, African language.

CLASPING AT CORDS
The *tsuzumi* is a small, waisted drum played in Japan. The cords that join the wide heads are gripped with one hand, which squeezes or releases the cords to vary the note.

DRIVING FORCE
The *tabla* is one of a pair of drums that drive along the *sitar* and *tambura* (pp. 40-41) in Indian music. The *tabla* player hits the centre of the skin with the fingers, while pressing down with the palm of the hand to vary the note.

ON THE OUTSIDE
This Nigerian rattle has strings of pellets fixed to the outside of a gourd.

Rattles

A rattle is simply shaken to make a sound. Many cultures used the rattle as part of traditional rituals, often to emphasize dance movements. Some rattles are simply strings of small, hard objects such as shells; others are made from pebbles, beads, and seeds inside a container.

HEAD-SHAKER
Carved in the form of a human skull, this gruesome, wooden rattle comes from North America.

RATTLE ON A STICK
Fruit shells filled with stones and mounted on a long stick make up this South African rattle.

MUSICAL OIL DRUM
Traditionally, the West Indian steel drum is made from an oil drum. Instead of a taut skin, it has a curved metal pan containing several panels that sound a different note when struck. A band contains a set of pans.

The *nungu* was beaten with a skin-covered stick called a *kapchen*

Metal jingle

MAGIC JINGLES
This unusual drum, seen from below, is the *nungu* from Siberia. The curious bits and pieces that hang from the bar are called *kungru*, and they jingle when the drum is beaten, rather like a tambourine. The *nungu* was played by a *shaman*, a priest whose magical powers de-pended on the number of *kungru* . The skin of the drum is decorated with red patterns that represent the upper and lower worlds. A drum in which a skin is stretched over a simple open frame like this is called a frame drum.

On the beat

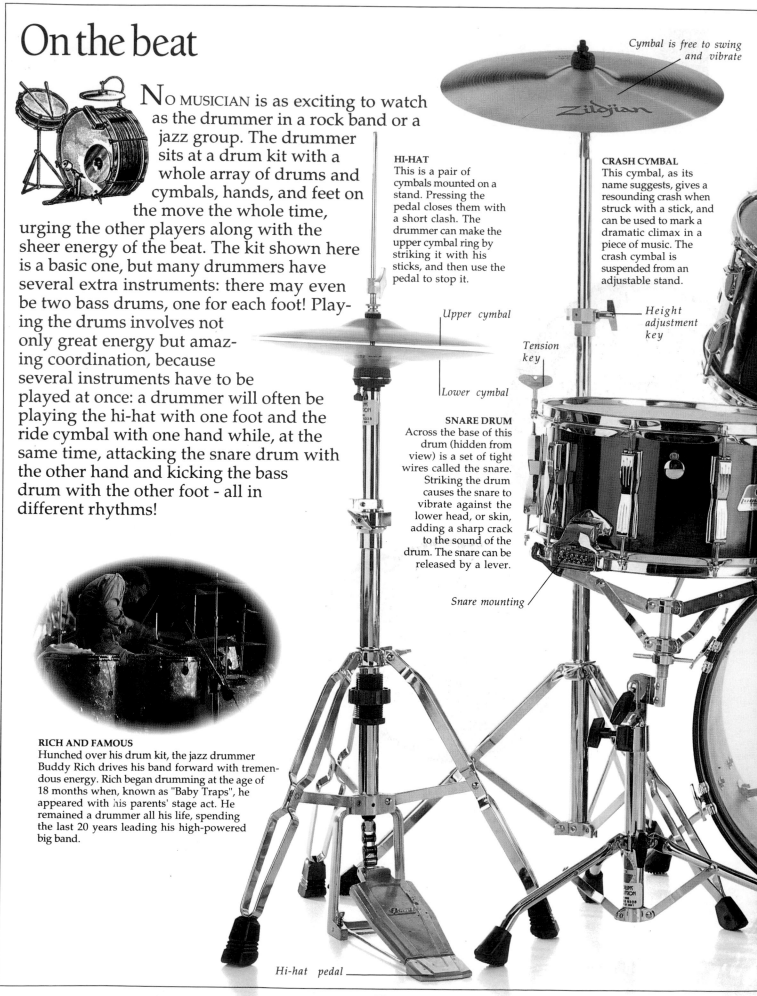

No musician is as exciting to watch as the drummer in a rock band or a jazz group. The drummer sits at a drum kit with a whole array of drums and cymbals, hands, and feet on the move the whole time, urging the other players along with the sheer energy of the beat. The kit shown here is a basic one, but many drummers have several extra instruments: there may even be two bass drums, one for each foot! Playing the drums involves not only great energy but amazing coordination, because several instruments have to be played at once: a drummer will often be playing the hi-hat with one foot and the ride cymbal with one hand while, at the same time, attacking the snare drum with the other hand and kicking the bass drum with the other foot - all in different rhythms!

RICH AND FAMOUS
Hunched over his drum kit, the jazz drummer Buddy Rich drives his band forward with tremendous energy. Rich began drumming at the age of 18 months when, known as "Baby Traps", he appeared with his parents' stage act. He remained a drummer all his life, spending the last 20 years leading his high-powered big band.

HI-HAT
This is a pair of cymbals mounted on a stand. Pressing the pedal closes them with a short clash. The drummer can make the upper cymbal ring by striking it with his sticks, and then use the pedal to stop it.

Upper cymbal

Lower cymbal

SNARE DRUM
Across the base of this drum (hidden from view) is a set of tight wires called the snare. Striking the drum causes the snare to vibrate against the lower head, or skin, adding a sharp crack to the sound of the drum. The snare can be released by a lever.

Snare mounting

Hi-hat pedal

Cymbal is free to swing and vibrate

CRASH CYMBAL
This cymbal, as its name suggests, gives a resounding crash when struck with a stick, and can be used to mark a dramatic climax in a piece of music. The crash cymbal is suspended from an adjustable stand.

Height adjustment key

Tension key

CAUGHT IN THE ACT
As this picture was taken, the drummer played a fast roll along four tom-toms mounted on a pair of bass drums. A rapidly repeating camera flash shows the sticks in action, revealing how evenly the drummer played.

Adjustable damper varies length of sound

TWO TOM-TOMS
Two tom-toms, or "toms", are mounted on the top of the bass drum. These small drums give high-pitched, mellow notes. They have a single head, which may be damped.

FLOOR TOM
This large tom-tom gives a deep resonant note. The drummer may use mallets to play the tom-toms, or strike them with the palms of the hands.

RIDE CYMBAL
This cymbal is often played with a stick to produce a "riding" rhythm.

Stick

Mallet

Brush (wire or plastic bristles)

BEATERS AND BRUSHES
Drummers mainly use sticks, brushes, or mallets to play the drums and cymbals. Sticks and mallets give the loudest sound, while brushes are quiet.

Bass drum pedal

BASS DRUM
The bass drum lies on its side and is played with a pedal connected to a felt-covered beater. It gives a short deep "thud".

Rubber feet grip floor firmly

Appeal of percussion

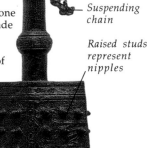

Notes as well as noises can ring out from percussion instruments. Striking bells of various sizes, or bars of wood or metal, gives a whole set of notes. Belltowers and carillons, which are the biggest instruments of all, send peals of notes and tunes cascading down to the streets below. At the other end of the scale, a few bars laid on a frame, or even across the player's legs, produce lovely, chiming sounds, resounding with music that is both tuneful and rhythmic at the same time.

Wooden beater

TWO-TONE
This double bell comes from West Africa. It is made of metal covered with fabric. The bells give two different notes when struck by the wooden beater.

Suspending cord

Suspending chain

Raised studs represent nipples

CHINESE CHIMES
Chimes go back to the Stone Age, when they were made from stone slabs. Shown here is a *po-chung*, from China. The bell is part of a chime, a group of bells suspended from a frame and struck with a stick. Seen as symbols of fertility, the bells were once used in temple ceremonies. Different notes were sounded to mark the seasons of the year.

Chime of gongs from Burma

BEATING THE BOSS
Unlike a bell, which produces the greatest vibrations when struck around the rim, the gong is suspended from its rim and struck at the centre. The whoosh of sound then vibrates from the central boss to the edges of the gong. While it may provide a signal - if only to dine - in orchestral music, the boom of a gong can be ominous. Gongs are popular in southeast Asia, and this elaborate example, decorated with fantastic beasts, comes from Borneo. They are often played in sets like the circular chimes of Thailand and Burma.

Beater with cork head

Central boss struck by beater

Leather strap is gripped in one hand

Clapper

HANDY CLANGERS
Handbells have been popular since the 12th century. These two come from a set of bells, each tuned to a different note of the scale. The bells contain a clapper that strikes the rim, making it vibrate with a "clang". Groups of bell-ringers play the bells by ringing in order.

High temple block

Medium temple block

Low temple block

Beaters

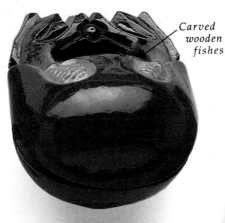

Carved
wooden
fishes

CEASELESS PRAYERS
Originating in China, these instruments
are called *mu-yus*, which means "wooden
fish". Carved to resemble fishes, the *mu-
yu* is symbolic of ceaseless prayer, because
fish never seem to sleep. They are also
called temple blocks.

TONGUE-TWISTER
Many instruments of South and
Central America originated in
Africa. This *sansa*, or thumb
piano, proves the link. It is
played by twanging the metal
tongues with the thumbs, so that
the various lengths give
different notes. The boat-shaped
body and carved head are
typically West African, but this
instrument comes from the upper
reaches of the Amazon.

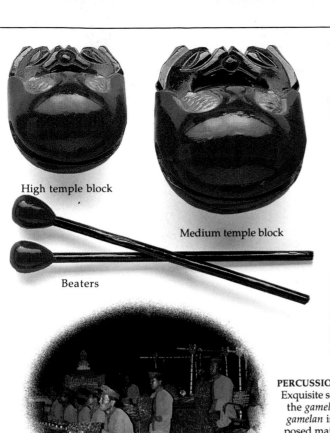

PERCUSSION ORCHESTRA
Exquisite sound is produced by
the *gamelans* of Indonesia. A
gamelan is an orchestra composed mainly of percussion instruments, each requiring great
virtuosity. It contains sets of
gongs and metallophones, which
are like xylophones but have
bronze bars set in ornate frames.

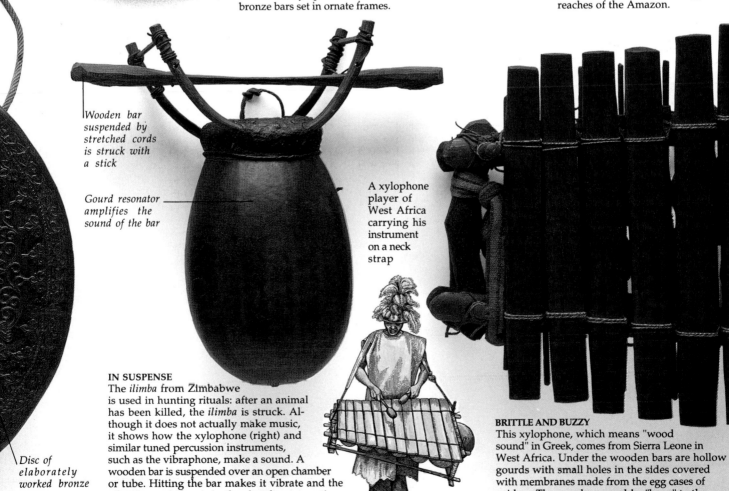

Wooden bar
suspended by
stretched cords
is struck with
a stick

Gourd resonator
amplifies the
sound of the bar

A xylophone
player of
West Africa
carrying his
instrument
on a neck
strap

IN SUSPENSE
The *ilimba* from Zimbabwe
is used in hunting rituals: after an animal
has been killed, the *ilimba* is struck. Although it does not actually make music,
it shows how the xylophone (right) and
similar tuned percussion instruments,
such as the vibraphone, make a sound. A
wooden bar is suspended over an open chamber
or tube. Hitting the bar makes it vibrate and the
vibrations set the air in the chamber resonating
with a hollow tone that amplifies the sound.

*Disc of
elaborately
worked bronze*

BRITTLE AND BUZZY
This xylophone, which means "wood
sound" in Greek, comes from Sierra Leone in
West Africa. Under the wooden bars are hollow
gourds with small holes in the sides covered
with membranes made from the egg cases of
spiders. The membranes add a "buzz" to the
sound of the xylophone.

Clang, crash, bang

NOISES PLAY an important part in many kinds of music: folk dancers often like to clap their hands in time to the music, for example, and many percussion instruments produce sounds that have no definite pitch or note. In much music, especially in South and Central America, musicians bang, shake, or scrape the kinds of instruments shown here. The lively rhythms of the sounds overlap to give a dancing beat that has terrific energy. Such "noises" can also be used to create moods. For instance, soft taps on a drum can sound menacing, while a drum roll is very dramatic.

Steel beads

Cog

Tongues

RATTLE OF GUNFIRE
Winding the handle of the cog rattle makes the cog strike the wooden tongues with a loud clatter. Beethoven used a cog rattle to simulate rifle fire in his *Battle Symphony*.

RATTLE OF STEEL
The *cabaca* (pronounced "cabassa") is a South American rattle with steel beads strung on the outside.

Police whistle

Train whistle

LITTLE BLOW-PEEP
A percussion player can blow short, shrieking blasts on a whistle to emphasize a rhythm while his hands are busy playing another instrument. Whistles also give sound effects: for example, the three-note whistle (right) sounds like a train whistle.

SEEDS AND BEADS
Maracas are pairs of rattles that come from South America. They are traditionally made of hollow gourds containing loose seeds, but can also be made of wood and filled with beads. Both hands are normally used to shake them.

Seeds inside hollow shell

HAND-SHAKER
Many percussion players in bands use shakers, which are hollow tubes containing loose beads (similar to maracas) and shaken in a lively rhythm. A small shaker can be gripped between the fingers while playing another instrument.

CUBAN CONCUSSION
These short wooden sticks are called claves or concussion sticks, and they come from Cuba. The two sticks are banged together to give a sharp "crack". Although this may sound easy, the timing of a rhythm has to be exactly right.

One stick is held with the hand cupped so the sound resonates

Jingle mounted in slot in frame

DROPPING A CLANGER
The tambourine is a small drum with jingles set into the frame. It is often decorated with ribbons, and can be held and played while dancing. The dancer taps the tambourine with the fingers, and shakes it or bangs it against the body. Another possible effect is a roll made by sliding a wet thumb around the rim. In his ballet Petrushka, Stravinsky directs the percussionist to drop a tambourine on the floor!

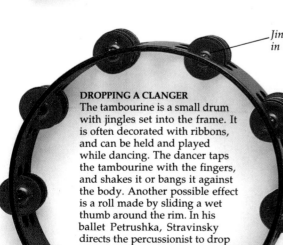

Pressing the top of each clapper sounds the castanets

HAND-CLAPPERS
Castanets are wooden clappers held in the hands. Orchestral players may use the castanet machine (above).

A pair of castanets is held together by a cord

Flamenco dancer with castanets

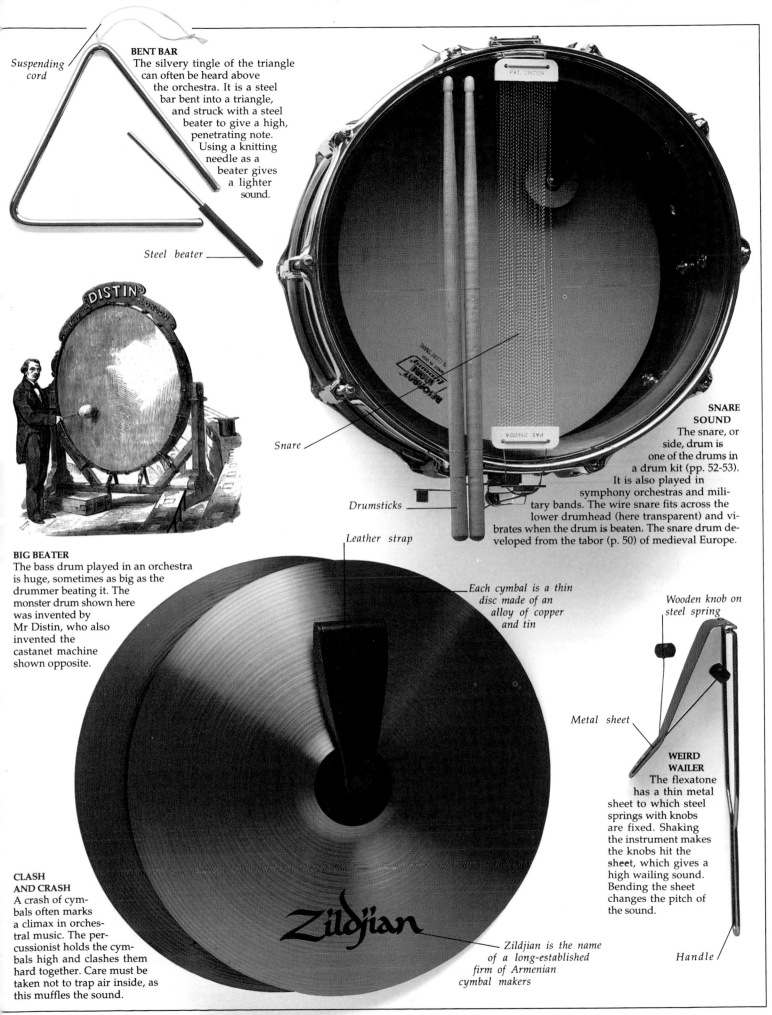

BENT BAR
The silvery tingle of the triangle can often be heard above the orchestra. It is a steel bar bent into a triangle, and struck with a steel beater to give a high, penetrating note. Using a knitting needle as a beater gives a lighter sound.

Suspending cord

Steel beater

BIG BEATER
The bass drum played in an orchestra is huge, sometimes as big as the drummer beating it. The monster drum shown here was invented by Mr Distin, who also invented the castanet machine shown opposite.

CLASH AND CRASH
A crash of cymbals often marks a climax in orchestral music. The percussionist holds the cymbals high and clashes them hard together. Care must be taken not to trap air inside, as this muffles the sound.

Snare

Drumsticks

Leather strap

SNARE SOUND
The snare, or side, drum is one of the drums in a drum kit (pp. 52-53). It is also played in symphony orchestras and military bands. The wire snare fits across the lower drumhead (here transparent) and vibrates when the drum is beaten. The snare drum developed from the tabor (p. 50) of medieval Europe.

Each cymbal is a thin disc made of an alloy of copper and tin

Zildjian is the name of a long-established firm of Armenian cymbal makers

Wooden knob on steel spring

Metal sheet

WEIRD WAILER
The flexatone has a thin metal sheet to which steel springs with knobs are fixed. Shaking the instrument makes the knobs hit the sheet, which gives a high wailing sound. Bending the sheet changes the pitch of the sound.

Handle

Electrifying music

Eᴌᴇᴄᴛʀɪᴄɪᴛʏ ꜰɪʀꜱᴛ ʙᴇɢᴀɴ ᴛᴏ ᴘʟᴀʏ ᴀ ᴘᴀʀᴛ ɪɴ ᴍᴜꜱɪᴄ with the advent of radio broadcasting early in the 20th century. Three elements are combined in order to make the music louder: a microphone or "pick-up" converts sound waves into electrical signals. These are then strengthened by an amplifier and passed to a loudspeaker - basically a glorified telephone earpiece - which changes the signals back into sound waves. This system can boost the quietest of noises, and electrified sound has a character all its own. The electric guitar was invented to overcome the limited volume of the acoustic guitar and now dominates popular music.

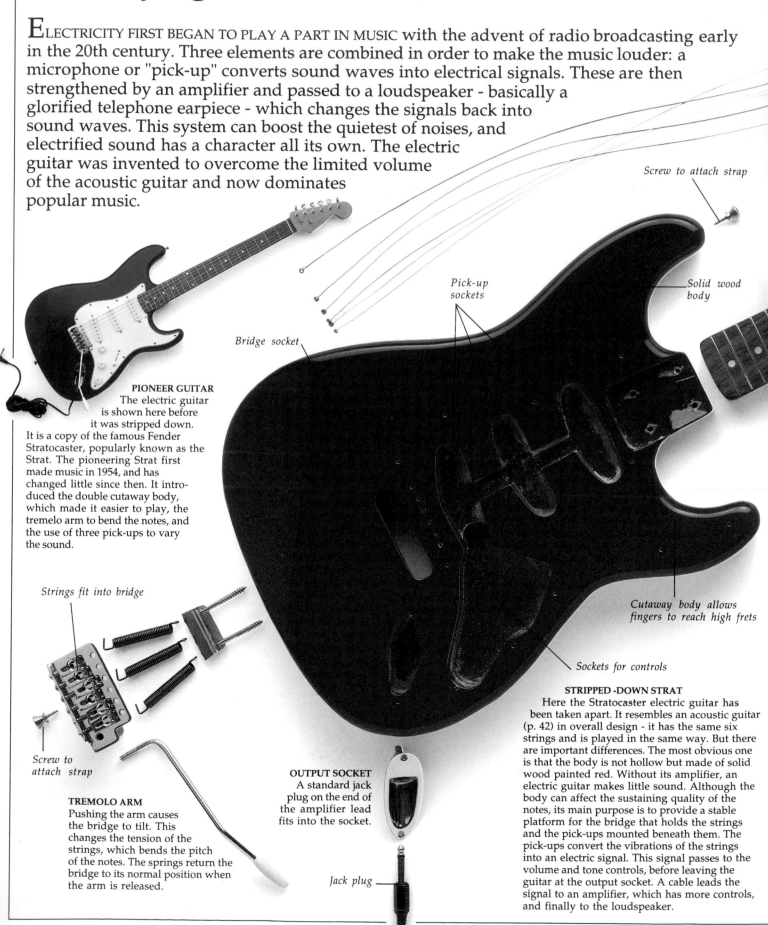

Screw to attach strap

Pick-up sockets

Solid wood body

Bridge socket

PIONEER GUITAR
The electric guitar is shown here before it was stripped down. It is a copy of the famous Fender Stratocaster, popularly known as the Strat. The pioneering Strat first made music in 1954, and has changed little since then. It introduced the double cutaway body, which made it easier to play, the tremelo arm to bend the notes, and the use of three pick-ups to vary the sound.

Strings fit into bridge

Cutaway body allows fingers to reach high frets

Sockets for controls

STRIPPED -DOWN STRAT
Here the Stratocaster electric guitar has been taken apart. It resembles an acoustic guitar (p. 42) in overall design - it has the same six strings and is played in the same way. But there are important differences. The most obvious one is that the body is not hollow but made of solid wood painted red. Without its amplifier, an electric guitar makes little sound. Although the body can affect the sustaining quality of the notes, its main purpose is to provide a stable platform for the bridge that holds the strings and the pick-ups mounted beneath them. The pick-ups convert the vibrations of the strings into an electric signal. This signal passes to the volume and tone controls, before leaving the guitar at the output socket. A cable leads the signal to an amplifier, which has more controls, and finally to the loudspeaker.

Screw to attach strap

OUTPUT SOCKET
A standard jack plug on the end of the amplifier lead fits into the socket.

Jack plug

TREMOLO ARM
Pushing the arm causes the bridge to tilt. This changes the tension of the strings, which bends the pitch of the notes. The springs return the bridge to its normal position when the arm is released.

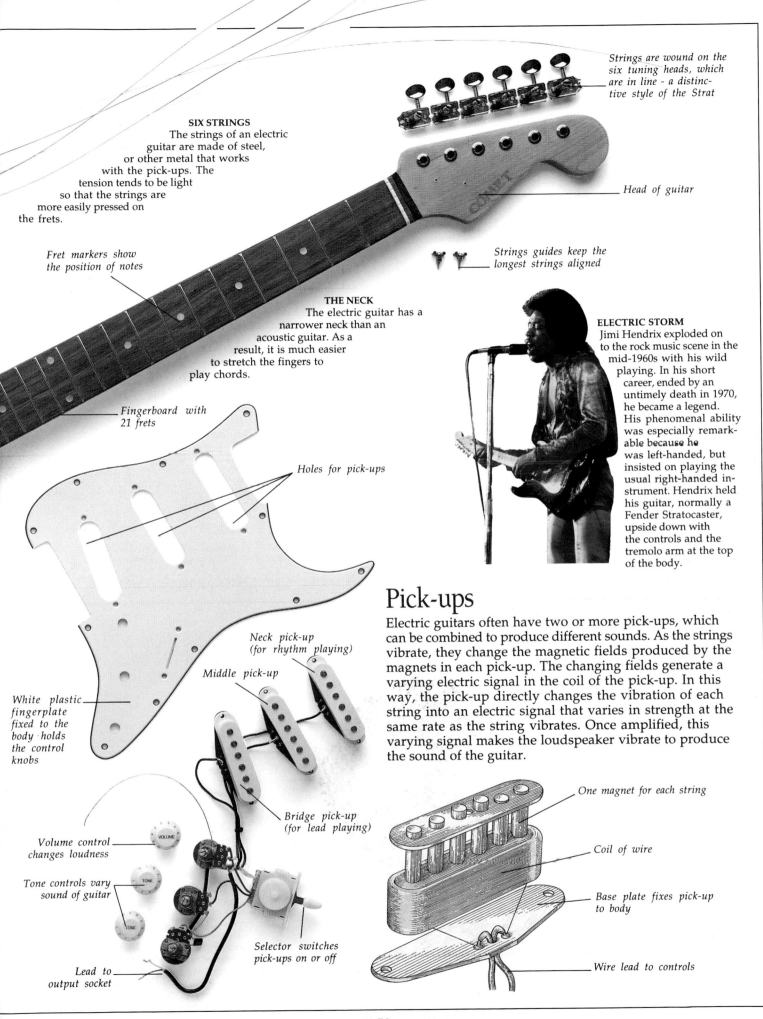

SIX STRINGS
The strings of an electric guitar are made of steel, or other metal that works with the pick-ups. The tension tends to be light so that the strings are more easily pressed on the frets.

Strings are wound on the six tuning heads, which are in line - a distinctive style of the Strat

Fret markers show the position of notes

Head of guitar

Strings guides keep the longest strings aligned

THE NECK
The electric guitar has a narrower neck than an acoustic guitar. As a result, it is much easier to stretch the fingers to play chords.

Fingerboard with 21 frets

ELECTRIC STORM
Jimi Hendrix exploded on to the rock music scene in the mid-1960s with his wild playing. In his short career, ended by an untimely death in 1970, he became a legend. His phenomenal ability was especially remarkable because he was left-handed, but insisted on playing the usual right-handed instrument. Hendrix held his guitar, normally a Fender Stratocaster, upside down with the controls and the tremolo arm at the top of the body.

Holes for pick-ups

Pick-ups

Electric guitars often have two or more pick-ups, which can be combined to produce different sounds. As the strings vibrate, they change the magnetic fields produced by the magnets in each pick-up. The changing fields generate a varying electric signal in the coil of the pick-up. In this way, the pick-up directly changes the vibration of each string into an electric signal that varies in strength at the same rate as the string vibrates. Once amplified, this varying signal makes the loudspeaker vibrate to produce the sound of the guitar.

Neck pick-up (for rhythm playing)

Middle pick-up

White plastic fingerplate fixed to the body holds the control knobs

Bridge pick-up (for lead playing)

One magnet for each string

Volume control changes loudness

Tone controls vary sound of guitar

Coil of wire

Base plate fixes pick-up to body

Selector switches pick-ups on or off

Lead to output socket

Wire lead to controls

Rock guitars

THE ELECTRIC GUITAR gives rock music its sound. Most bands have two - often three - electric guitars. These are: a lead guitar that plays the solos, a rhythm guitar to play rocking rhythms behind the lead and the singer (often the same person), and a bass guitar that pumps out a driving bass line to urge the band forward. Add the power of the drum kit (pp. 52-53) to all this electricity, and you have rock music in all its various forms. Because the solid body of an electric guitar does not produce the actual sound that is heard, it can be made in any shape that can be held. Rock guitars can come in a bizarre range of shapes, colours, and materials, but most stars put music first and prefer the more standard styles.

In this early model the strings pass through the back of the body

V-FORMATION
The Gibson company pioneered the electric guitar, introducing the first one in 1935. This was basically a Spanish model fitted with a pick-up, and was called the Electric Spanish. In 1957 Gibson brought out the humbucker pick-up, which has two coils to prevent hum. The famous Gibson Flying V guitar dates from 1958, when the company brought it out to revive its flagging fortunes. The futuristic style of the body was successful even though it was awkward to hold while play-ing. This particular instrument is an early 1958 Flying V, and it is now a collector's piece.

Twin humbucker pick-ups give fat sound characteristic of Gibson guitars

Solid wooden V-shaped body

Output socket

Bigsby tremolo arm

BEATLE MANIA
The Beatles were the most successful rock group of the 1960s. They had the classic rock line-up of two electric guitars (George Harrison on lead guitar and John Lennon on rhythm guitar - see above), bass guitar (Paul McCartney) and drums (Ringo Starr).

NOT-SO-SOLID ROCK
Not all electric guitars have solid bodies. Many are semi-acoustic guitars that have hollow bodies with f-shaped soundholes, like those in the violin (p. 32). The Gretsch 6120 semi-acoustic guitar was made famous by Eddie Cochran. This particular guitar dates from 1957, and bears the name of the country music star Chet Atkins on the finger-plate. It has a Bigsby tremolo arm, an alter-native design to the Fender arm introduced on the Stratocaster guitar (p. 58).

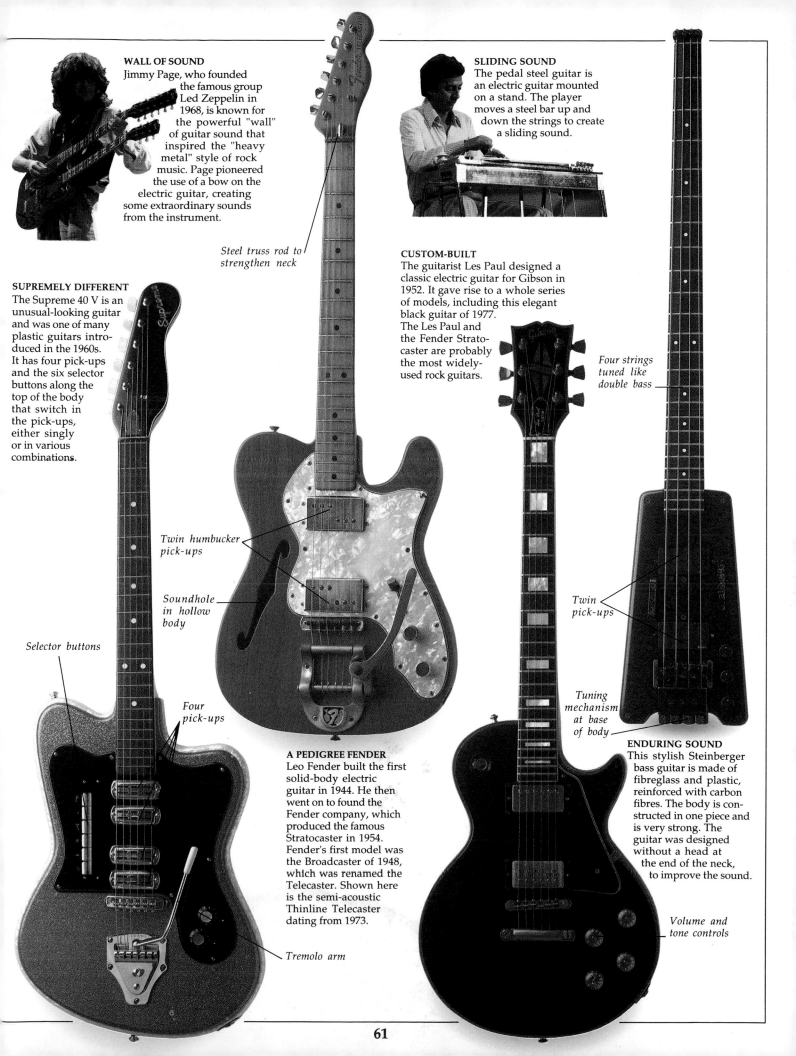

WALL OF SOUND
Jimmy Page, who founded the famous group Led Zeppelin in 1968, is known for the powerful "wall" of guitar sound that inspired the "heavy metal" style of rock music. Page pioneered the use of a bow on the electric guitar, creating some extraordinary sounds from the instrument.

SLIDING SOUND
The pedal steel guitar is an electric guitar mounted on a stand. The player moves a steel bar up and down the strings to create a sliding sound.

Steel truss rod to strengthen neck

SUPREMELY DIFFERENT
The Supreme 40 V is an unusual-looking guitar and was one of many plastic guitars introduced in the 1960s. It has four pick-ups and the six selector buttons along the top of the body that switch in the pick-ups, either singly or in various combinations.

CUSTOM-BUILT
The guitarist Les Paul designed a classic electric guitar for Gibson in 1952. It gave rise to a whole series of models, including this elegant black guitar of 1977. The Les Paul and the Fender Stratocaster are probably the most widely-used rock guitars.

Four strings tuned like double bass

Twin humbucker pick-ups

Soundhole in hollow body

Selector buttons

Twin pick-ups

Four pick-ups

A PEDIGREE FENDER
Leo Fender built the first solid-body electric guitar in 1944. He then went on to found the Fender company, which produced the famous Stratocaster in 1954. Fender's first model was the Broadcaster of 1948, which was renamed the Telecaster. Shown here is the semi-acoustic Thinline Telecaster dating from 1973.

Tuning mechanism at base of body

ENDURING SOUND
This stylish Steinberger bass guitar is made of fibreglass and plastic, reinforced with carbon fibres. The body is constructed in one piece and is very strong. The guitar was designed without a head at the end of the neck, to improve the sound.

Tremolo arm

Volume and tone controls

Machine music

THE MUSIC OF THE FUTURE may well consist of sounds made by machines. The synthesizers, and other electronic instruments shown here, do not make their own sounds; they produce an electric sound signal that goes along a cable to an amplifier and loudspeaker - like an electric guitar (pp. 58 - 59). These machines can make many different kinds of sound signals, giving a wide range of sounds. They can imitate other instruments or conjure up entirely new sounds. The computer is important in electronic music because it can control music-making machines and even create the music that they make.

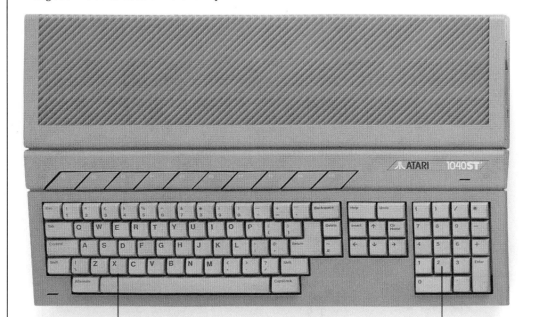

Pad contains electronic components under the surface

PADS FOR DRUMS
Drummers can become electronic musicians with a kit of drum pads. Hitting the pad with a stick makes the pad produce an electric sound signal that gives an electronic drum sound.

Standard drumstick

ONE-MAN BAND
Popular music makes great use of electronic sounds. One of the pioneers is the French musician Jean-Michel Jarre. He was one of the first musicians to create an electronic orchestra in which he performed all the music himself. This can now be done easily by a computer.

COMPUTER CONTROL
This is an ordinary home computer which, among its many other uses, can be linked to electronic instruments like those shown here. Music software on small discs enables the computer to store, process and create musical notes. It can be turned into a recording studio; it can correct wrong and mis-timed notes and even compose.

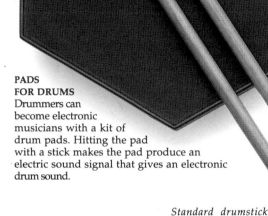

Software to record 60 different sounds

Software makes the computer compose music

ELECTRONIC KEYBOARD
This synthesizer is played like a piano or organ. It can produce all kinds of real and unusual sounds by operating the controls above the keys. The display shows which sounds have been chosen. Not all guitar synthesizers are played like guitars but plucking the strings gives a wide range of electric sounds.

Standard keyboard

Number keys

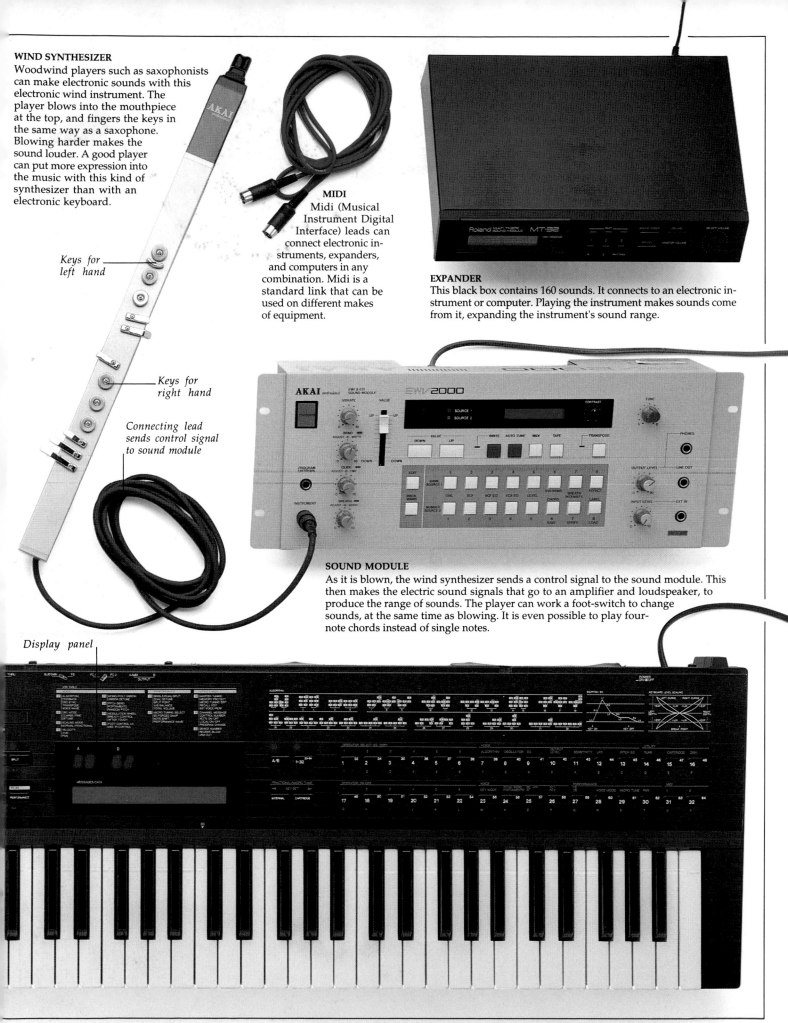

WIND SYNTHESIZER
Woodwind players such as saxophonists can make electronic sounds with this electronic wind instrument. The player blows into the mouthpiece at the top, and fingers the keys in the same way as a saxophone. Blowing harder makes the sound louder. A good player can put more expression into the music with this kind of synthesizer than with an electronic keyboard.

Keys for left hand

Keys for right hand

Connecting lead sends control signal to sound module

MIDI
Midi (Musical Instrument Digital Interface) leads can connect electronic instruments, expanders, and computers in any combination. Midi is a standard link that can be used on different makes of equipment.

EXPANDER
This black box contains 160 sounds. It connects to an electronic instrument or computer. Playing the instrument makes sounds come from it, expanding the instrument's sound range.

SOUND MODULE
As it is blown, the wind synthesizer sends a control signal to the sound module. This then makes the electric sound signals that go to an amplifier and loudspeaker, to produce the range of sounds. The player can work a foot-switch to change sounds, at the same time as blowing. It is even possible to play four-note chords instead of single notes.

Display panel

Index

Acknowledgments

Dorling Kindersley would like to thank:
Horniman Museum, London, also Dr Frances Palmer and the staff of the Musicology Department for their assistance.
Pitt Rivers Museum, University of Oxford, also Dr Hélène La Rue and the staff of the Ethnomusicology Department for their assistance.
Phelps Ltd, London, also Rachel Douglas and Gerry McKensie for their assistance.
Hill, Norman and Beard Ltd, Thaxted, also Andrew Rae and Richard Webb for their assistance.
Bill Lewington Ltd, London; Boosey and Hawkes Ltd, London; Empire Drums and Percussion Ltd, London; Simmons Electric Percussion Ltd, London; Vintage and Rare Guitars Ltd, London John Clark; Adam Glasser; Malcolm Healey; Chris Cross; John Walters for the loan of equipment and assistance.
Janice Lacock for extensive editorial work on the early stages of the book.
Tim Hammond for editorial assistance.
Lynn Bresler for the index.
Jonathan Buckley for his help on the photographic sessions.
Tetra Designs for making the models photographed on pp. 6-7.

Picture credits
t=top b=bottom m=middle l=left r=right

J. Allan Cash Ltd: 19t, 24m, 50r, 51l, 56b:
E.T. Archives: 8tl
Barnaby's Picture Library: 13br, 17tr
Bridgeman Art Library: 12tl, 16b, 21lm, 26b, 29r, 30t, 30m, 35tr, 36tr, 38t, 40m, 50b,
Douglas Dickens: 55m
Mary Evans Picture Library: 6r, 10tl, 11tr, 11m, 15tr, 18m, 19b, 20tr, 22tl, 24b, 26t, 29t, 34tr, 36tl, 37b, 38l, 46m, 46b, 50tl & c, 54tl, 54m, 57m
Fine Art Photographic Library Ltd: 6mr, 22tr, 36bl, 42t
John R. Freeman: 29b
Sonia Halliday Photographs: 18t, 36b
Robert Harding Associates: 6bl, 39t, 41t
Michael Holford: 8tr, 28tl, 36m, 37m
Hutchinson Library: 42r, 38m
Image Bank: 6tr, 53t
London Features International Ltd: 59r, 61tl, 62
Mansell Collection: 16tl, 17m, 20b, 21rm, 24t, 30l
John Massey Stewart: 28mr, 37tr
National Gallery: 44l
David Redfern: 23m, 52l, 60m, 61tl
Sefton Photo Library: 14m, 13br, 22l
Thames and Hudson Ltd: 46t
Topexpress: 48bl

Illustrations by Coral Mula, Will Giles and Sandra Pond. Picture research by Millie Trowbridge.

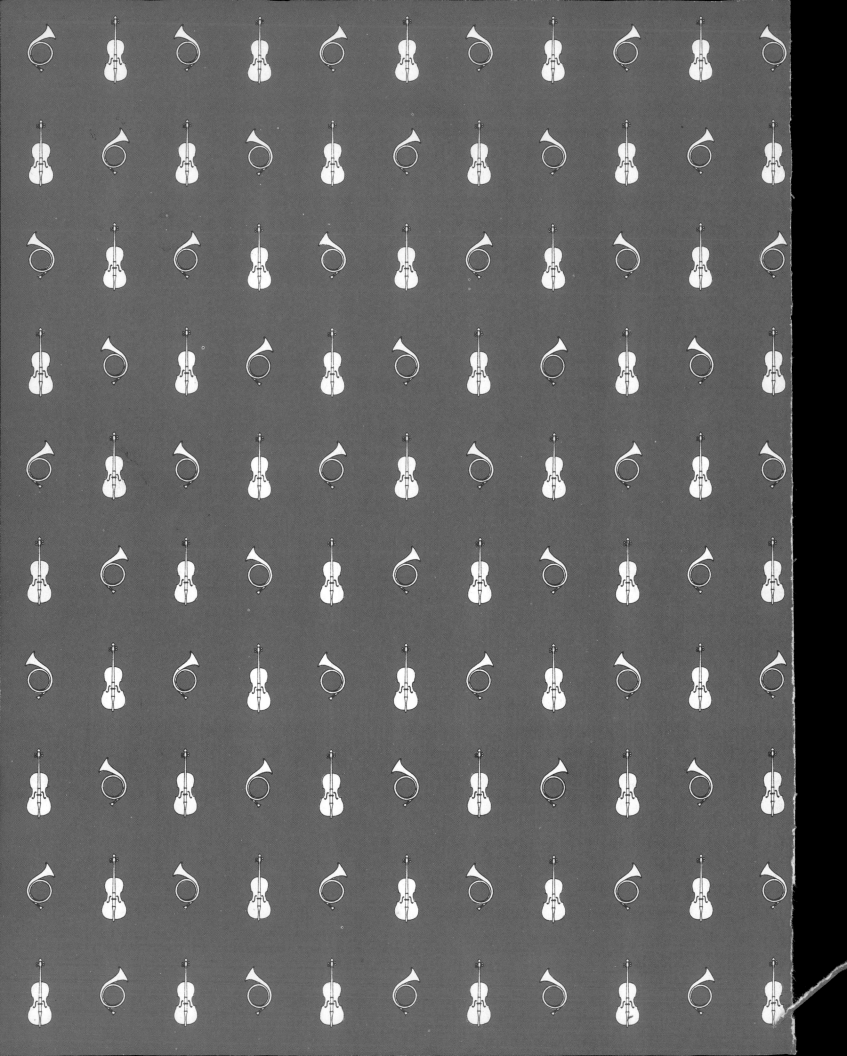